DATE DUE			
JUN 1 6 1999			

CLEMENCEAU
and the Third Republic

CLEMENCEAU
and the
Third Republic
by
J. HAMPDEN JACKSON

HYPERION PRESS, INC.
Westport, Connecticut

Published in 1946 by Hodder & Stoughton, London
Hyperion reprint edition 1979
Library of Congress Catalog Number 78-14127
ISBN 0-88355-800-9
Printed in the United States of America

Library of Congress Cataloging in Publication Data
Jackson, John Hampden, 1907-
   Clemenceau and the Third Republic.
   Reprint of the 1946 ed. published by Hodder & Stough-
ton, London in series Teach yourself History library.
   Bibliography
   Includes index.
   1. Clemenceau, Georges Eugene Benjamin, 1841-1929.
2. France—History—Third Republic 1870-1940.   3. States-
men—France—Biography.   I. Series: Teach yourself history
library.
DC342.8.C6J3   1979   944.081'092'4   78-14127
ISBN 0-88355-800-9

A General Introduction to the Series

THIS series has been undertaken in the conviction that there can be no subject of study more important than history. Great as have been the conquests of natural science in our time —such that many think of ours as a scientific age *par excellence*—it is even more urgent and necessary that advances should be made in the social sciences, if we are to gain control of the forces of nature loosed upon us. The bed out of which all the social sciences spring is history; there they find, in greater or lesser degree, subject-matter and material, verification or contradiction.

There is no end to what we can learn from history, if only we would, for it is coterminous with life. Its special field is the life of man in society, and at every point we can learn vicariously from the experience of others before us in history.

To take one point only—the understanding of politics: how can we hope to understand the world of affairs around us if we do not know how it came to be what it is? How to understand Germany, or Soviet Russia, or the United States —or ourselves, without knowing something of their history?

There is no subject that is more useful, or indeed indispensable.

Some evidence of the growing awareness of this may be seen in the immense increase in the interest of the reading public in history, and the much larger place the subject has come to take in education in our time.

This series has been planned to meet the needs and demands of a very wide public and of education—they are indeed the same. I am convinced that the most congenial, as well as the most concrete and practical, approach to history is the biographical, through the lives of the great men whose actions have been so much part of history, and whose careers in turn have been so moulded and formed by events.

The key idea of this series, and what distinguishes it from any other that has appeared, is the intention by way of a biography of a great man to open up a significant historical theme; for example, Cromwell and the Puritan Revolution, or Lenin and the Russian Revolution.

My hope is, in the end, as the series fills out and completes itself, by a sufficient number of biographies to cover whole periods and subjects in that way. To give you the history of the United States, for example, or the British Empire or France, *via* a number of biographies of their leading historical figures.

That should be something new, as well as convenient and practical, in education.

GENERAL INTRODUCTION

I need hardly say that I am a strong believer in people with good academic standards writing once more for the general reading public, and of the public being given the best that the universities can provide. From this point of view this series is intended to bring the university into the homes of the people.

A. L. ROWSE.

ALL SOULS COLLEGE,
    OXFORD.

Contents

Introduction

THE story of Clemenceau's life is inseparable from that of France throughout sixty crucial years. From the birth of the Third Republic to within a decade of its death he played a central part in every public crisis. When the Prussians were besieging Paris and the revolutionary Commune was proclaimed he was mayor of Montmartre ; when Bismarck's peace-terms were being discussed he was a member of Parliament, opposing capitulation; when France was repairing the ravages of defeat and civil war he was president of the Paris Municipal Council. During the formative years of the new Republic he was leader of the unofficial Radical opposition in Parliament—from 1876 to 1893—and during the moral crises of the last years of the century he was at the centre of the Boulanger, Panama and Dreyfus affairs. When industrial strikes and German menaces intensified in 1906 he became head of a ministry which lasted longer than almost any other in the Third Republic. When defeat at the hands of Germany seemed imminent in 1917 he became Prime Minister again and led France to victory. He was chairman of the Paris Peace Conference and principal author of the Treaty of Versailles. In 1920, in his seventy-ninth year, he resigned, but even then his public work was not over, for in 1930 his last book was published forecasting the ruin that was to come upon France and indicating a way to salvation.

In more senses than one Clemenceau was the central figure of the Third Republic. His most courageous battles were fought for a middle path. Members of the general public are so used to associating a middle path with weak conciliation and boneless compromise that they often fail to recognize a positive central policy when they see one. Clemenceau was anything but conciliatory and he hated compromise. At the peril of his life he strove for a middle way between the revolutionaries of Paris and the bourgeois of Versailles, between the socialists and the reactionaries, between the appeasers and the avengers, between the defeatists and the jingo adventurers, between trust-Germany pacifists and decimate-Germany militarists. Public memory has come to think of Clemenceau as the Tiger, the extremist, the protagonist of revenge. It is an ironic fate for a man whose first important parliamentary speech was a plea for amnesty for the Communard prisoners and whose last published work was an attack on the man who wanted to separate the Rhineland from Germany.

In character, as well as in policy, Clemenceau was a central figure. His realism, his logic and his wit, his pugnacity, his distrustfulness and his malice are all in the grand tradition which has been labelled French ever since those qualities

xii

were first exemplified in Voltaire two centuries ago. The very paradoxes of his character—in which contempt was combined with kindness, cruelty with pity, frivolity with moral purpose, individualism with patriotism—cease to be paradoxes when they are seen to be French. The range of his interests as shown in his writing is French in its catholicity and in its limitations; for Clemenceau, who would have been famous as a publicist if he had never made a speech or held a public position, turned his mordant pen not only to politics but to medical science and to rationalist philosophy, to Impressionist painting and to Ibsenite drama, and to the interpretation of daily life in the primitive Vendée and in sophisticated Paris. His character lay at the centre of gravity of France—though gravity is an odd word to use in connection with Clemenceau.

To understand Clemenceau is to understand France. Not the whole of France; there are important aspects of the French tradition which were foreign to him: the religious and mystic France, the Roman and Gothic France were beyond his range. What he typifies is the prevailing France as the world has known her during the last hundred years. He had the essence of Republican France in him, as Churchill has the essence of aristocratic England.

Chapter One

The Making of a Man

THE Clemenceau family had lived in the
Vendée for centuries. In the early days
they were yeoman-farmers, working the land
they owned, but as time went on they came to own
rather more and to work rather less, until they
had leisure. Unlike the neighbouring squires,
some of them devoted their leisure to intellectual
pursuits. Being of a practical turn of mind, the
Clemenceau men turned to the study of medicine:
there was an apothecary in the family in the
seventeenth century, and the great-grandfather,
the grandfather and the father of Georges
Clemenceau were all doctors. None of them
practised much. They were thoughtful country
gentlemen first and doctors second. Tending the
ailments of the peasantry soon taught them that
disease is not to be cured by pills or probes.
Poverty was at the root of one-half of the ills
from which the peasants suffered, and ignorance
crossed with superstition was at the root of the
other half. The Vendée was one of the most
backward and priest-ridden provinces of France;
a political purge would be needed to give it
health. So the Clemenceau men turned to

politics. They were Radicals at the time of the Revolution, when one of their cousins, Laré-veillière-Lepeaux, voted in the Convention for the death sentence on the King and took part in the stamping-out of the Catholic and Royalist insurrection in the Vendée. The grandfather of Georges Clemenceau was a Jacobin and the father, Dr. Benjamin, was a Republican, notorious for his opposition to King Louis-Philippe and to the Emperor Louis-Napoléon, and still more notorious for his atheism.

The family seat was the Château de l'Aubraie, a moated mediæval castle buried in the woods near Féol. For one reason or another—possibly because he was quarrelling with his bucolic brother Paul, possibly because he thought a crumbling castle no place for a confinement—Dr. Benjamin sent his wife back to her parents' house in the village street of Mouilleron-en-Pareds for her lying-in, and there on September 28th, 1841, their first son was born. He was given the names of Georges Benjamin, but not in baptism. Dr. Benjamin did not believe in the sacraments of the Church and none of his six children was baptized. The district was shocked, but the Clemenceau family was too highly respected on other grounds for this to lead to social ostracism. The child played with the other village children on an equal footing, and the growing boy who rode to and from the Château de l'Aubraie never seemed other than

2

a typical Vendéen. The castle was more than half a farm-house and its inhabitants were not far from being farmers. Though eccentric in their ideas, their behaviour followed a pattern that was well understood in the Vendée. Georges Clemenceau was never to be without honour in his own country.

It is not hard for us to imagine the background against which the boy was reared. There were squireens in the West of Ireland not so long ago living much the same sort of life as the Clemenceau family lived in the West of France in the 1840s—careless, spacious, uncomfortable lives in tumble-down country houses where the best quarters are given over to the horses and the only warm room beyond the kitchen is the library ; lives that are the alternate delight and despair of the tenantry and the unmitigated despair of the priest. It would be absurd to push the parallel too far, but one cannot think of the salient characteristics of Clemenceau—his independence of mind, his anti-clericalism, his agin'-the-government individualism—without recalling certain sons of Irish Ascendancy families who have done so much to leaven the lump of our democracy.

Clemenceau himself in later years ascribed these characteristics to the *genius loci.* " Our dear *bocage* with its granite, its ravines, its lakes, its quiet valleys cut off from the world—all dominated by the slopes of the Alouettes mountain with their view of the towers of Nantes and the

3

lights of La Rochelle and Rhé. . . . How can I deny that I owe to the nature of the Vendée the best of the inimities which I have managed to gather on my way through life: the instinct for independence, freedom of criticism, obdurate obstinacy, combativeness? Those who blame us for these virtues, which are so unpleasing to oppressors of every sort, perhaps forget that thanks to our combative nature we and our Breton cousins formed the last square of the Celts, of the Gauls, to hold out against the armies of Rome and the hordes of Germania." But it was more particularly to his family that Clemenceau owed his characteristics. His father, Dr. Benjamin, was of independent means, and although his ancestors had worked for a living, they had never, as far as memory could reach, worked for a master. Of the attitudes of mind that came of being an employee—the servility, the timorousness, the occasional passionate revolt— no Clemenceau knew anything. Being doctors, they understood poverty and could recognize many of the failures of the will and spirit that bring ruin to a man, but they understood nothing of the employee-relationship. Not understanding servility, or its twin-offspring flattery and spite, they could never forgive it. This was to be a source of weakness, as well as of strength, to Clemenceau throughout his career.

To be against the Government seemed as natural to a Clemenceau as to be independent, but there was nothing facile about their opposition to Church and State. In a Protestant or in an irreligious society it is easy and inglorious to defy the clergy; in the Vendée of a century ago it was almost heroic. In a democratic society it is not costly to oppose the government; in the France of Louis-Napoléon it might be fatal. When Clemenceau was sixteen, a curly-headed schoolboy at the Lycée of Nantes, he was suddenly brought up against the political facts of life by the arrest of his father. The Government, alarmed by Orsini's attempt on the life of the Emperor, had ordered a round-up of " disaffected persons," and the Nantes police could think of nothing better than to raid a bookshop where the Republican intellectuals of the town were in the habit of meeting for discussion. Dr. Clemenceau was held for a month in the town-gaol before being sentenced, without trial, to deportation. By the time the manacled prisoner had reached Marseilles, such a protest had been raised by all parties in Nantes that the Government thought it best to release him. The doctor returned home unperturbed, but the episode left an impression on his children that none of them was likely to forget.

Back in the Vendée, the doctor found Georges ready to learn from him in a way that few sons are ready to learn from their fathers. (The story goes that on the terrible morning when his father was waiting handcuffed for the prison van, the boy had run up to him with the words: " I will avenge you." The reply was: " If you want to avenge me, work.") They took long walks together, discussing the family philosophy. Its outlines were very simple. They had been best expressed in the Declaration of the Rights of Man in 1789. " Men are born free and equal in rights; social distinctions can be founded only on usefulness to the community. The aim of all political institutions is the preservation of the natural and permanent rights of man; these rights are liberty, property, security, and the right to resist oppression. . . . Liberty consists in the power to do anything which does not harm others. Thus there are no limits to each man's natural rights other than those which ensure that the other members of society enjoy those same rights. These limits can be determined only by law. . . . The law is the expression of the general will; all citizens have the right to contribute personally or through their representatives to its formation; it must be the same for all, whether to protect or to punish. . . . Nobody may be distrained upon because of his opinions, even religious opinions, provided that their manifestation does not disturb public order as established by law."

These principles, as Dr. Clemenceau explained to his son, France had never found a way of applying. Ten years of revolutionary upheaval left the people with such a desire for security that

6

they welcomed Bonaparte in the hope that he would restore order. Bonaparte's dictatorship was followed by defeat, and defeat by fifteen years of reaction under the restored Bourbons. The French rose against the legitimate Bourbons and replaced them by Louis-Philippe, a more bourgeois King of the Orléanist branch, who ruled as a constitutional monarch with the support of the merchant princes; but he never succeeded in giving the people their rights, least of all their economic rights. Louis-Philippe was thrown out by a rising of liberal intellectuals and Paris workers on February 24th, 1848, but the Second Republic thus established could not satisfy the impatient masses who demanded security and order as well as liberty. They voted for a nephew of Bonaparte, Louis-Napoléon, who promised to be a more democratic edition of his uncle. Louis-Napoléon soon became an Emperor, and now, in 1859, he was ruling France as dictator. Seventy years had passed since the Declaration of the Rights of Man, and the problem was still how to apply those principles to France, how to complete the unfinished Revolution.

The discussion between father and son continued on a more philosophic plane. In Dr. Clemenceau's philosophy atheism was blended with a belief in the perfectibility of man through scientific knowledge and moral effort. He had learned much from the English Philosophic

7

Radicals and two books just published in England were to set his mind in a ferment of excitement. John Stuart Mill's *On Liberty* and Darwin's *The Origin of Species* fitted exactly into the traditional Clemenceau outlook. To a speculative biologist like Dr. Benjamin, Darwin's work was particularly exciting. It seemed to confirm the basic theories of Auguste Comte, his favourite French thinker. Comte had described the history of thought as going through three stages—the theological stage which referred everything to an external God, the metaphysical stage which saw reality in abstract ideas, and the Positivist stage which draws conclusions from experience and observation of positive, scientific facts. The positive approach, insisted Comte, must be taken to all sciences, particularly to biology and to its sequel sociology, the science of society. So far father and son were agreed: neither had any use for theology or metaphysics and both were naturally Positivists; and if the aberrations of Comte's later works fell nothing short of madness, it was interesting and important to work out exactly when the great man had departed from sanity.

When Georges was nineteen the time had come for him to go to Paris and work for his degree. He was to be a doctor, of course, but not a mere medical practitioner; a Clemenceau must make science the basis of philosophy and philosophy the basis of social action. Auguste Comte had

8

proffered a theoretic pattern, and there were working models among Dr. Benjamin's own acquaintances—men like Blanqui, the insurrectionist whom he had once helped to escape, and Michelet, the poor printer's son whose works were giving the French people a new belief in themselves through a popular interpretation of their history; younger men like Arthur Ranc, the Republican journalist who had shared Dr. Benjamin's imprisonment, and Etienne Arago, the scientist whose good looks and vigour seemed to mark him out as a leader of men. The boy would be in good hands in Paris.

Equipped with an adequate allowance and with a letter of introduction to Arago, Clemenceau took lodgings in the Quartier Latin and began his student life. It was the life of Murger's *Scènes de la vie de Bohême*, but sweetened by money and stiffened by intelligence. Paris in 1860, with the Second Empire at the height of its gas-lit glory, was a liberal education for any young man; for Clemenceau it was very heaven. He was fascinated by the theatre, as well he might be, for Dumas *fils* and Augier were pouring new wine into the old bottles of social comedy, and Sardou was winning his first triumphs. He was fascinated, with equally good reason, by the new novels. Flaubert was beginning to be known, and Alphonse Daudet and the brothers de Goncourt were bringing out their first books. As for philosophy, it was moving in precisely the direc-

9

tion which a Clemenceau was best fitted to appreciate: the philosophers were quarrying their theories out of scientific experiment and were moving towards the new science of sociology.

At the same time the ferment of political thought was reaching a fresh intensity. The ideas of 1789 were now seething again; they had never ceased to work below the surface and had bubbled up in 1848 when political democracy and economic socialism were realized to be means to the goal of Liberty, Equality, Fraternity. Seeing the movement in the vats, the Emperor Louis-Napoléon decreed a few reforms tending in the direction of parliamentary government. These reforms were enough to keep the moneyed men and even the labouring masses quiet, but the Left-wing journalists took them to be a dangerous sop and continued to distrust the Emperor's intentions. In their opinion the time had come for another revolution like that of February 24th, 1848, when the monarchy had fallen like the walls of Jericho. The Quartier Latin pullulated with ephemeral journals advocating Republicanism. Among these appeared a little paper called *Le Travail* with articles signed Méline and Floquet, verses signed Zola, and literary and dramatic criticism signed Georges Clemenceau.

Le Travail was nothing if not provocative. The stunt of the moment was to organize a procession through Paris to commemorate the fourteenth anniversary of the February revolution. The editorial staffs of the Republican papers were to participate. This brought Clemenceau into the hands of the police and eventually got him sentenced to a month's imprisonment. It was not a romantic experience. The detention period and the prison sentence did not run concurrently; altogether Clemenceau spent seventy-three days in Mazas gaol, during which, he afterwards said, he suffered as much boredom as if it had been seventy-three years.

He emerged bursting with pent-up energy which he wisely devoted to his medical studies. Professor Charles Robin found him an exemplary pupil and helped him with his doctoral thesis on the Generation of Anatomic Elements. It was a description of current medical research and is interesting chiefly for its attitude towards the Comtists' doctrines on biological origins. Materialist generalization, wrote the young Clemenceau, could provide no answer to the mystery of life: "We are not among those who hold with the Positivist school that science can provide any answer to the enigma of things."

A great deal of work must have gone into this thesis, but there was always time for other interests. From the courtyard of the hospital, Clemenceau could see the window of the cell where Blanqui was imprisoned. He visited Blanqui regularly for the best part of a year. The legendary leader of a hundred attempts at insurrection was a cantankerous old man, sick and ravaged with jealousy of his fellow revolutionaries. He took to Clemenceau and set him impossible tasks involving smuggled printing-presses and kidnapping. The student bore with him; he knew a hero when he saw one, and although there was no hero-worship in his constitution he warmed to the patriotism in Blanqui which remained constant throughout all insurrectionary fantasies.

The real bent of Clemenceau's mind, however, was not towards medicine, revolutionary conspiracy, or even towards the theatre (Sarah Bernhardt had just made her début at the Comédie Française; it was a great age for a dramatic critic). Its direction can be seen by his action in the early spring of 1865 when, as soon as he had taken his final medical examination, he went straight to England. "I arrived at dawn in the Christian city of London, and I saw the steps of the houses and pavements littered with pitiable creatures of all ages and of both sexes, trying to sleep in the frosty night air." His destination was John Stuart Mill's house in Blackheath. He was still following in his father's footsteps. What interested him above all was social philosophy, particularly the brand of Radicalism which Mill had made his own. Mill had exposed the Utilitarians' fallacy of the greatest good of the greatest number: the greatest goods are not material. He had exposed the Utopian *simplisme* of the French Socialists: all social processes are

12

infinitely complex and reform depends on the improved characters of individuals. Liberty to Mill meant the fullest, least fettered development of the individual; equality meant not uniformity but its opposite, diversity. At the same time there were certain reforms that should be fought for immediately, certain legal and economic injustices that must be redressed. All this was meat and wine to the young Clemenceau. And Mill's latest work seemed a direct continuation of the discussions which he had had with his father. Mill had just published in the *Westminster Review* a study on " Auguste Comte and Positivism " in which he stressed the value of Comte's philosophy of history and ranked him as a thinker with Descartes and Leibnitz, but poured justified ridicule on the mania for systemization shown in Comte's later work. Clemenceau got Mill's permission to translate this study into French. Then, with the essay in his valise and interviews with Herbert Spencer and Frederic Harrison in his head, he went home and astonished his parents by announcing that he intended to sail immediately for New York.

America was in the throes of revolution and civil war. Lincoln had decreed the abolition of slavery, and the armies of the slave-owning South were at last being pressed back by the Northerners under Grant. Here was political philosophy in action, a combination which it was not in Clemenceau to resist. Washington and

13

New York were drawing him by the same attraction that Leningrad and Moscow were to exert on young men two generations later; he must have felt with Mill that the American struggle " was destined to be a turning-point, for good or evil, of the course of human affairs for an infinite duration." His father was more than a little doubtful about the project. It was all very well for Clemenceau to say that he wanted to study America according to the Positivist method, but why need he order such very expensive clothes— including a pair of black satin breeches and a frock coat costing 100 francs ? It was all very well for him to insist that he was following in the wake of de Tocqueville, but why be in such a desperate hurry ? With considerable misgivings, Dr. Benjamin gave his paternal blessing: " If you are a serious-minded man (*sérieux*), which it is my duty to assume until I have proofs to the contrary, you will be able to make your profession, which assures you a living, assist your political career. So go to America. Come back as well informed in politics as you are in medicine, and then get down to work."

But was Clemenceau *sérieux* ? His first letters' home were reassuring. He was working on his translation of Mill. He had struck up a friendship with Horace Greeley, the editor of the New York *Tribune*, who had led the campaign for the abolition of slavery. These were good signs, but even better was to be found in the

14

political correspondence which he was contributing to *Le Temps*. He had arrived at New York in the middle of the reign of terror which followed the assassination of President Lincoln at the moment of the Northerners' victory. There were corruption and vindictiveness everywhere. Clemenceau visited Tammany Hall and learnt how far corruption could go. He went to Florida and witnessed some of the worst negro-lynchings. The evidence he saw of decay of moral fibre throughout the Union was enough to drive to cynicism any young man who had gone out with Clemenceau's rosy vision of the war and its probable outcome, yet he wrote with insight and balance in *Le Temps*. Writing before slavery was abolished legally by the Thirteenth Amendment to the Constitution and while lynchings were at their height, he said: " Slavery is a thing of the past in America where the most refined and cultivated people used to defend it so excellently. In the Southern plantations that I visited they proved to me that slavery is in the Bible, and nothing could be more true. . . . " Writing in 1865 when Reconstruction had been turned into an excuse for jobbery and victimization, he prophesied: " Everywhere one looks there are political and social difficulties to be seen here, but fortunately there is in the United States an indescribable faculty for adaptation to circumstances, for accepting the lessons of experience, for rapidly changing direction; thanks

15

to this, pessimistic forecasts almost always prove unfounded. Mistakes will certainly be made, but means will always be found for rectifying them. There will be long flounderings in the void of incomplete, tentative solutions, but these people will always end by seeing where justice and truth lie. . . . Let us reserve our judgment for a while." Three years later, when Grant had succeeded Johnson as President, he gave his judgment in *Le Temps*: " Men pass, but principles remain. A question not settled justly is eternally open. With the passing of Johnson and the advent of Grant, unity returns to this Government; the executive and the legislative powers begin again to work in unison; the radical party finds the field free before it, and the revolution continues its victorious advance."

All this was promising enough in a man of twenty-four, but his father's worst suspicions seemed confirmed when Clemenceau wrote home hinting that he intended to settle in the United States. It was all very well to go to America to study democracy as a newspaper correspondent at 150 francs a month, but no serious Frenchman could contemplate living permanently outside France. Dr. Benjamin took a stern tone in his reply and went so far as to cut off his son's allowance by way of bringing the puppy to heel.

Nettled by the implication that he was incapable of earning his living, Clemenceau promptly found a part-time job as teacher of French in Miss Aitken's Academy for Young Ladies at Stamford, Connecticut. Here he enjoyed himself far too much. Between riding out from New York on Monday mornings and returning two days later, he found time to teach French by the direct method, accompanying the young ladies on their picnics and infatuating them by his conversation and horsemanship. He was riding for a fall. He had forgotten that rich American Misses were not Parisian Musettes. An affair with a pupil could have no consummation but marriage, and marriage was what he offered Mary Plummer. The child—she was hardly more—was an orphan. Her guardian, a Protestant pastor, naturally insisted on a Church wedding, which was more than Clemenceau had bargained for. The young atheist sailed superbly off to France.

This might have been his salvation, but Clemenceau was in no mood to learn wisdom. It was a tragedy that his best friend, Jourdain, had died while he was away. Twenty years his senior and a man of great penetration and balance, Jourdain might have had a steadying influence. " You know your great fault," he had written to Clemenceau, in the early New York days, " I remind you of it without ceremony. Men were made for you to walk beside, not to trample over, aristocrat that you are." In truth Clemenceau was consumed with arrogance, and

17

looked it. Contemporary portraits bring out the disdainful eyes, the short egoistical nose and the truculent lips only half-hidden by a black moustache and beard. While in Paris he made a reputation as a dandy and fought his first duel. He was restless and impatient, waiting for a letter from the Plummers waiving the point about a Church wedding. As soon as it arrived he returned to America and on June 23rd, 1869, in the New York City Hall, he was married to Mary. He was twenty-seven, his bride nineteen; they had nothing in common. The marriage was doomed from the start, although the pair were to be bound together for seven years and were to have three children—two daughters and a son—before the inevitable separation.

Marriage is no evidence of maturity. Clemenceau was still not grown up. His life so far had been a splendid preparation for something, but he had no idea for what. He had proved his courage, physical and moral, in a duel and in successful battles of will against his father and against his wife's people, but these were hollow triumphs. He was a fully qualified doctor, but medicine was not his vocation. He had studied the political thought and had met the leading republicans and democrats of three nations, but he had not the temperament to be a student or even a reporter of politics. The thought of Emperor Louis-Napoléon and his ducal advisers and archducal protégés made him burn with

18

anger. " Good heavens, yes, those people are
always charming," he had written to a woman
correspondent in September 1867. " We know
that beforehand; they have been charming for
five or six thousand years. They have got the
recipe for all the virtues, the secret of all the
graces. Do they smile ? Then it's delightful.
Do they weep ? How touching! Do they let
you live ? What exquisite kindness! Do they
crush the life out of you ? It's the misfortune of
their situation. Very well, I am going to tell
you something: all those Emperors, Kings, Arch-
dukes and Princes are grand, superb, generous
and sublime; their Princesses are anything you
wish; but I hate them, I hate them with a merci-
less hatred as people used to hate in the old days
of 1793 when that poor fool of a Louis XVI used
to be called the execrable tyrant." This mood
of angry hatred persisted in Clemenceau. It was
a symptom of frustration rather than of direction
in life.

By the autumn of 1869 he was back in the
Vendée with his bride, living in his father's house
and dividing his time between riding about the
countryside and practising medicine at a shilling
or two a visit. The four years in America had
left him out of touch with political developments
in France. He did not realize how much progress the republican movement had been making
in Paris. Some of the workers had begun to
organize themselves in trade unions; an office of

19

the Marxist International had been opened; Blanqui, though still in prison, was making converts. At the same time republican ideas were spreading among the professional classes. Radical criticism of religion and morals, of society and the State, was no longer confined to students in the Quartier Latin. The little Leftist journals were becoming a force in the capital, thanks to the corrosive pen of Henri Rochefort, whose weekly paper, *La Lanterne*, had a sale of 120,000 copies. A great orator had emerged in the person of a young barrister, Léon Gambetta. Rochefort and Gambetta were a link between the working-class revolutionaries and the middle-class radicals. The elections of May 1869 returned these hotheads to parliament, together with nearly forty other Republicans. But Louis-Napoléon had no intention of leaving France with a choice between revolutionary Republicanism and imperial dictatorship. He aimed at a middle way, made some changes in the Constitution in the direction of a parliamentary régime, and invited the public to approve his reforms in a plebiscite. By a majority of six million votes to one million France declared herself satisfied with the reforms.

Clemenceau found nothing in all this to lift him out of his mood of angry frustration. He was fretting for an opportunity for action. It came more suddenly than anyone could have imagined. On July 18th, 1870, Louis-Napoléon was manœuvred by Bismarck into declaring war against Prussia.

War! The news that filtered through to the West was confusing: the French Imperial troops were winning glorious victories, but they abandoned Alsace; they were bound to win, but they had let the Prussians shut up Bazaine's army in Metz; they had the finest light arms in the world—the chassepôt rifle and the mitrailleuse—but these were useless against the Prussian field artillery. Clemenceau left his wife at l'Aubraie and hurried to Paris, where he took lodgings with Lafont, a friend of his student days, in Montmartre. Here he got a clearer picture of the war. The French troops were ill-disciplined and badly, though bravely, led. The Emperor, who had assumed supreme command of the forces in the field, was a dying man and his entourage rotten. The war could still be won by France, but not—if Arthur Ranc and Etienne Arago and other members of the republican opposition were to be believed—by the Imperial Government.

On the night of Saturday, September 3rd, a rumour ran round Paris: the Emperor's army had capitulated at Sedan and Marshal MacMahon and the Emperor himself were prisoners! On Sunday morning the unbelievable news was confirmed by the Council of Ministers. A bewildered crowd surged round the Palais-Bourbon, where Parliament was in session. Clemenceau and Arthur Ranc found themselves inside the building at the moment when Jules Favre and Gambetta, the Opposition leaders, were proclaiming the end of the Empire.

The end of the Empire! But what could take its place? Only a Republic, only a régime on the lines of the First Republic which had saved France from the invader eighty years ago. The crowd swung away to the Hôtel de Ville to hear the new Republic proclaimed by Favre and to carry by acclamation the appointment of a new Government of National Defence. The President, inevitably, was a general, Trochu. His politics were anything but Republican and his military record was not distinguished, but he had published a pamphlet on the reform of the army, and anyhow he was Governor of Paris and the best general available at the moment. The ministers, naturally, were the Parisian leaders of the parliamentary opposition to the Empire, and since the elder statesmen among them, notably Thiers, preferred to keep in the background, the chief ministries were taken by the younger deputies, with Jules Favre as Minister of Foreign Affairs and Gambetta, who was scarcely older than Clemenceau, in the key position as Minister of the Interior.

This meant that Clemenceau's friends were in power. The new Government had no authority beyond the acclamation of the mob, but it had no rival. Not one man's hand was raised in Paris to save the Empire, not one shot was fired.

There was not even need to shed a drop of imperialist blood ; the Empire had vanished away. Gambetta nominated Arago as Mayor of all Paris with orders to clear the old mayors out of the twenty municipal boroughs (arrondissements) and to replace them by sound republicans. Arago put Clemenceau in charge of the eighteenth arrondissement, that of Montmartre. The new mayor lost no time in placarding the narrow streets of the Butte with a proclamation. " Citizens," it ran, " must France destroy herself and disappear, or shall she resume her old place in the vanguard of nations? It is this question we are called upon to answer to-day. The enemy is at the gates of the city. The day may not be far distant when our breasts will be the last rampart of the mother-country. Each of us knows his duty. We are children of the Revolution: let us seek inspiration in the example of our forefathers in 1792, and like them we shall conquer. Vive la France! Vive la République! " Clemenceau had found himself.

Chapter Two

The First Crisis : 1870-71

TWO tasks faced France in the autumn of
1870: she had to drive out the invader and
she had to make a Revolution. Neither seemed
impossible to the people of Paris. In their eyes
the two were complementary: the war had won
the Republic and the Republic could win the
war. Although one army had been lost at Sedan
and another was surrounded in Metz, the
Germans would have to tie up 200,000 of their
troops round Metz and another 250,000 round
the vast circumference of Paris. There would be
time to organize new armies on the Loire and in
the South. It would mean improvising, but had
not the armies which had saved France in 1792–
93 been improvised ? The Republic would again
be the salvation of France. In place of the
elderly professional soldiers and jaded conscripts
of the Empire, the Government of National
Defence would command new men, knowing
what they were fighting for and loving what they
knew. In place of the hidebound Imperial
bureaucrats, who had denied self-government
even to Paris, the greatest, most civilized city in
the world, France would be led by zealots whose

24

administration would be backed by the united will of the people.

This optimism was soon to fade. In beleaguered Paris military organization and civil administration alike suffered from too much zeal. Each of the twenty arrondissements made its own arrangements for distributing the diminishing stocks of food. There was no effective control of prices and for some time there was no general rationing system. The rich could get food and the poor could not; even the slaughtered animals of the Zoo were sold at prices which the ordinary housewife could not afford. Normal work was at a standstill, and the only alternative to unemployment was service in the National (Home) Guard, where any man who could raise a rifle could enrol at fifteen pence a day. The Paris National Guard soon reached the astonishing figure of 360,000 men. But again each arrondissement made its own arrangements. In working-class districts, where patriotism amalgamated with revolutionary ardour in a fulminous compound, the National Guard legions were bitterly opposed to those of the richer districts and were suspicious not only of the nominal commander of the Paris National Guard, General Clément Thomas, but also of the head of the Government, General Trochu, and of the regular army units which he was regrouping behind the city fortifications. The National Guard legions each elected a Vigilanc Committee to keep an eye on their

superiors. A central committee of these vigil-
antes issued a programme on September 14th:
"To take measures for the security of the country
as well as for the definitive foundation of a truly
republican régime by the permanent co-operation
of individual initiative and popular solidarity."
Thus, revolution and national defence were to go
hand in hand, leaving only one arm free for the
organization of victory.

The capital was now cut off by the German
siege from the rest of France. There was no
communication except by dirigible balloons which
were at the mercy of every breeze, and by carrier
pigeons which had an unaccountable way of
getting lost. The masses were not long in realizing that there was no co-ordinated plan of
campaign. General Trochu had never been a
Republican: it was now realized that he was not
even a strategist. After October 8th, when
Gambetta left the city by balloon to make contact
with the armies of the provinces, there was a
suspicion in Paris that the remaining members of
the Government of National Defence were betraying both the country and the Revolution. These
suspicions became certainty after October 28th,
when the septuagenarian statesman Thiers, who
had long been execrated by the working class,
entered Paris with a pass from Bismarck, bringing
the news that Bazaine's army had surrendered
and Metz had fallen. Thiers had satisfied himself that France could look for no help from
26

England or from Russia. He came with Bismarck's offer of an armistice, and might have won the Government's consent to it but for the action of working-class Paris. Clemenceau was echoing the spirit of all Montmartre when he proclaimed: " The Municipality of the Eighteenth Arrondissement indignantly protests against an armistice, which the Government cannot accept without betraying its trust." On October 31st the Vigilant Committees of the East-end districts led a mob to the Hôtel de Ville where they demanded the resignation of the Government and its replacement by a group of their own insurrectionary leaders. Jules Favre saved the ministers' skins by promising to hold municipal elections and to take no punitive action against the demonstrators. But there could be no question now of negotiating with Bismarck. The war must go on, in the desperate hope that Gambetta's armies could raise the siege before Paris was starved.

In these appalling circumstances the Mayor of Montmartre made his district a model of good administration. Montmartre at that time was still more or less isolated from the city that lay below the hill; it had only recently been incorporated in the city boundary and was a strange mixture of independent-minded provincial town and suburban slum. The war changed its complexion: evacuees from the centre came crowding on to the Butte for safety. With no census of the population and no inventory of supplies to guide

27

him, Clemenceau organized the distribution of food and fuel, set up a chain of relief-centres and first-aid points and reopened the schools. He concentrated on the schools for medical as well as educational and political reasons. By re-opening them under lay control, he secured not only Republican teaching but the proper distribution of milk and clothes and the general welfare of the children while their mothers were out working and their fathers busy with the defence of Paris. His duties were military as well as civil. He had to raise and equip recruits for the new Republican Army as well as for the local legion of the National Guard. Yet he had no military rank and no legal authority until the municipal elections of November 8th confirmed him in his mayoralty.

For the full discharge of his responsibilities Clemenceau could depend on nothing but the goodwill of the people of Montmartre. For a time this was enough. Throughout the four long months of the siege, the coldest winter within living memory—when the Parisians were huddling in cellars at night under the Prussian bombardment, queueing outside the empty shops by day, raging against the rich who had money and stores, against General Trochu (the name, it was said, derived from *trop choir*) who had a plan but nothing to show for it—Clemenceau ruled his little province on the hill and discovered, in his thirtieth year, powers of leadership and of applica-

28

tion to detail such as even Arago had not suspected in him.

Before the end of January, though Paris still held out, the war was lost. One after the other, Gambetta's armies had been defeated—at St. Quentin, at Le Mans, at Héricourt. Bismarck celebrated his triumph by proclaiming the King of Prussia to be Emperor of Germany, thus founding the Second Reich in the Galerie des Glaces at Versailles, on January 18th. On January 26th Jules Favre accepted Bismarck's terms for an armistice, pending the election of a National Assembly with authority to conclude a peace. Gambetta resigned, hoping that his gesture would secure the return of deputies committed to continued resistance. It did nothing of the sort. The National Assembly elected in haste on February 8th was overwhelmingly, and naturally, defeatist. Soldiers absent from their constituencies could not vote; in the forty-three departments occupied by the Germans no public meetings were allowed. Only in Paris was there any political activity, and only in Paris was there a strong vote for defying Bismarck. In the provinces the voters wanted peace at almost any price which would enable them to get rid of the Germans and to resume their normal life. Few people outside Paris felt any gratitude towards the Republicans. Their Government of National Defence had failed to defend the nation. If it had not been under the thumb of the Paris

29

mob it could have had much better terms from
Bismarck than were available now, after three
months of costly resistance. Thiers had been
right. The provincials voted for solid, sensible
deputies—country gentlemen, members of the
professions, men of substance—and Thiers was
returned in more than twenty constituencies.
The new National Assembly consisted of 630
deputies, of whom 400 were conservative monarchists, 30 Bonapartists in the Louis-Napoléon
tradition and 200 Republicans in traditions that
defy classification. At Bordeaux, after a bitter
debate on March 1st, only 107 deputies voted
against peace-preliminaries and opposed the
cession of Alsace-Lorraine to Bismarck's new
German Empire. Clemenceau, who had been
elected by 96,000 grateful Parisians, was among
them. The friend of Gambetta and the enemy
of Thiers, he had to see the latter installed as
virtual dictator of France, subject only to the
good offices of Bismarck.

When Clemenceau returned to Paris a few
days after the Bordeaux vote, he found the city
in an uproar. The Germans, in accordance
with the preliminary peace-terms, had made a
ceremonial march down the Champs-Élysées
before returning to their camps on the northern
outskirts of the city. They preferred to leave
Thiers to deal with the unsubdued Parisians.
Thiers' action was not conciliatory. He declared
Versailles to be the new capital and arranged for

the Assembly to move there from Bordeaux. He appointed Imperial officers as heads of the Army, the police and the National Guard, and he added injury to insult by lifting the moratorium on bills and rents, thus leaving the Parisians faced with financial ruin. The Parisians construed all this as a prelude to the restoration of a monarchy and of despotic rule. In the working-class districts the people were determined not to surrender either to the Germans or to the reactionary Government of Thiers. Clemenceau realized that there was imminent danger of a civil war from which no one but Bismarck would stand to gain.

The immediate issue centred round some guns which the National Guard had saved from the Prussians by hauling them up from the artillery parks in Passy and the Place Wagram to the heights of Montmartre and Belleville. Under the terms of the armistice, Thiers was bound to remove them from Paris. Clemenceau, believing that this would certainly lead to a breach between Paris and the Government, got him to promise to wait. Given time, it might be possible to bring Paris and Versailles to an understanding. But Thiers was in a hurry: he suddenly sent General Lecomte up to Montmartre with a body of troops to haul away the guns.

March 18th, 1871, was the most memorable day in Clemenceau's life. He was awakened at six o'clock by the news that the Buttes had been

31

occupied. Hurrying up the hill through the raw fog, he found General Lecomte waiting about for tackle and transport. The streets were calm—it was still an hour before dawn—and there was no sign of resistance, though Clemenceau found a sentry lying wounded, and dressed his injuries while telling Lecomte that now he was here he had better get the guns away quickly or there would be trouble. For the moment there was nothing more to be done, and Clemenceau went down to his Mairie. There, soon after eight o'clock, he heard the call-to-arms sound over Paris and, looking out of his window, saw the square filling with National Guards. They were dragging the famous guns by hand. Soon after he heard that the Guards had interned General Lecomte and some other officers and police who had offered resistance.

Clemenceau's only care now was to prevent bloodshed. He paid for food to be taken to the prisoners and detailed a National Guard Captain (Mayer) to be responsible for their safety. He knew the danger of his own position: the National Guards already suspected him of working on behalf of the Government, and the Government would certainly suspect him of conniving at insurrection. What he did not know was that insurrection had spread all over Paris, and that the National Guard had set up a revolutionary government, with power in the hands of their own Central Committee. One of the local com-

32

mittees was actually in session in a room at the Montmartre Mairie where Clemenceau came upon them at three o'clock and ordered them unceremoniously out.

An hour and a half later the crisis came. Captain Mayer burst into the Mairie shouting to Clemenceau: " They are going to shoot the Generals "—meaning Lecomte and Clément Thomas who had been found strolling about in civilian clothes and had been shut up with the other prisoners. The Mayor grabbed his sash of office and ran up the hill again, this time through frenzied crowds hurling insults at him and shrieking that Lecomte and Thomas had been shot. At the top he saw some National Guards leading other officers to the courtyard of Scribe's old house in the Rue des Rosiers. Clemenceau barely had time to intercede with them when bedlam broke loose. The incident is best described in his own words:

" Suddenly a terrific noise broke out, and the mob which filled the courtyard burst into the street in the grip of some kind of frenzy. Amongst them were chasseurs, soldiers of the line, National Guards, women and children. All were shrieking like wild beasts without realizing what they were doing. I observed then that pathological phenomenon which might be called blood-lust. A breath of madness seemed to have passed over this mob: from a wall children brandished indescribable trophies; women, dishevelled and

33

emaciated, flung their arms about while uttering raucous cries, having apparently taken leave of their senses. I saw some of them weeping while they shrieked louder than others. Men were dancing about and jostling each other in a kind of savage fury. It was one of those extraordinary nervous outbursts, so frequent in the Middle Ages, which still occur amongst masses of human beings under the stress of some primeval emotion."

How Clemenceau escaped murder at the hands of that mob he never quite knew. Wearing his sash of office in which he symbolized the Government against which the insurrection was aimed, he walked steadily down the Rue de la Chausée-Clignancourt. "If a single man had uttered to my face certain definite accusations that were in the minds of all, thousands of voices would have been raised against me, and it is my profound conviction . . . that I should have suffered the fate of the Generals." Something in his mien prevented the outburst. Clemenceau regained his Mairie, where, at the centre of the storm, all was quiet.

The position now was that the Central Committee of the National Guard was installed in the Hôtel de Ville as the actual but illegal Government of Paris, in opposition to the legal Government under Thiers which had moved out of the city to Versailles where the National Assembly was sitting. Clemenceau had been

34

unable to prevent an insurrection, but it might still be possible to avert a civil war. He went out to Versailles on March 21st to take his seat in the Assembly, and there, in conjunction with Ranc and some other Paris mayors, he put forward a programme of compromise, asking for " Recognition of the Republic, the right of Paris to govern herself by a Council freely elected, with full control over her police, finance, teaching and public welfare, and the entrusting of the protection of Paris to the National Guard composed of all valid electors."

This was too much for Versailles and not enough for Paris. The mayors' proposal aroused such an outcry in the Assembly that the president, unable to preserve order, was obliged to terminate the session, and Clemenceau returned to Paris saying, " They don't want to understand anything or to do anything." In Paris elections held for a Communal Council on Sunday, March 26th, resulted in a victory for the extremists and disaster for the compromisers. Clemenceau was defeated, only 700 votes being cast for him in Montmartre. Three-quarters of the members of the new Commune were unmitigatedly Red.

It is difficult to say what their redness implied. By calling themselves the Commune they echoed the revolutionary fervour of 1793 and seemed to promise a Terror, or centralized government of intimidation, in the name of the working people. But the name also echoed the ideas of Proudhon

35

and indicated a decentralized France composed
of a federation of autonomous communities.
Some of the leaders, such as old Delescluse, were
Jacobins in the 1793 tradition; others, such as
Beslay, the first President of the Commune, and
Courbet, the President of its Guild of Artists,
were federalist disciples of Proudhon. There was
no unity among the Communards; they were not
in any sense a party. Some were gentle idealists,
some were brutal fanatics, many were adventurers
and a few were crooks; none were Marxists in
the modern sense. Most of them were very
young (the average age of the Executive Committee of the Commune was under thirty-seven)
and not one of them had any experience of
governing. The movement they led was com-
pounded of simple patriotism which refused to
admit German victory, of pride in Paris which
could not accept the subordination of the city to
any National Assembly, and of the revolutionary
élan of the forgotten men, of the artisans who saw
at last a possibility of government of the people,
by the people, for the people.

For a week after its election the Commune
seemed to have a chance of success. Thiers had
only 22,000 troops at his command; he admitted
later that these were the worst days of his life:
" If we had been attacked by 70,000 or 80,000
men, I should not have wanted to answer for
the stability of the army." But with the news
that Communard insurrections had failed in
36

Lyon and in the southern cities, and that Bismarck was releasing prisoners to supplement the army of reaction which Thiers was organizing at Versailles, civil war became certain and defeat inevitable. On April 2nd the Versailles troops advanced on Courbevoie and shot its prisoners. On April 3rd the Communard forces made their first sortie along the roads to Versailles. " One would have said that it was a band of turbulent holiday-makers," wrote their sympathetic historian Lepelletier, " setting out gaily and uncertainly for the country, rather than an attacking column directing itself towards a formidable opposition." They advanced without artillery or ambulance services, and the main columns chose a road passing beneath the guns of Fort Mont-Valérien, which was held by the Versailles troops. The sortie failed ignominiously, the Communards racing back for the shelter of Paris like a picnic party before a thunder-storm. A second siege of Paris began, a siege organized by Thiers under the pardonably gloating smiles of the Germans who were at St. Denis.

Clemenceau still worked furiously for compromise. His group of Paris mayors and deputies, calling themselves the League of Republican Union for the Rights of Paris, issued a manifesto on April 6th: " It has proved impossible to avoid civil war. The refusal of the Versailles Assembly to recognize the legitimate rights of Paris has led inevitably to bloodshed. We must now see to it

37

that this struggle, which brings consternation to the heart of every citizen, does not have as its result the loss of the Republic and of our liberties." Then followed the programme of the League in terms identical with those which Clemenceau had heard submitted to the Assembly two long weeks ago—recognition of the rights of Paris to local self-government and to its own independent National Guard.

The manifesto was signed by Floquet, Lockroy, Allain-Targé, Clemenceau and other men who were to be famous as Radicals in later years. Their programme might have become the basis for a compromise peace if events had brought a stalemate between Versailles and the Commune, but Thiers had no intention of letting things get to that pass. Every week saw his army stronger and better equipped and his mind more determined on the extermination of the Communards. The League of Republican Union had a hope—a very faint hope—of finding a basis for reconciliation by rallying the provinces round Gambetta's ideal of a united Republic. They arranged for a Congress to be held at Bordeaux, and on May 10th Clemenceau and four other delegates set out from Paris—Clemenceau with a borrowed American passport. Thiers forbade the Congress (what else could he do? It would be an open breach of the Armistice with Bismarck) and sent his police to round up the delegates on their return to Paris. Clemenceau's colleagues walked into

38

the trap and were arrested. He himself out-
witted the police by taking a train in the Strasbourg direction. When he reached the St. Denis
gates of Paris after this detour he found them
barricaded and guarded by Prussian soldiers:
the Versailles troops were in the city and the
worst carnage in the history of civil war had
begun.

Thiers' troops, many of them illiterate Bretons
who thought they were fighting a Catholic
crusade, had broken into Paris in the night of
May 21st through the open West-end suburbs.
The Communard fighters—one can hardly call
them soldiers—were driven back from barricade
to barricade, setting fire to buildings to cover their
retreat, until they reached the line of the Rue
Royale and the Boulevard St. Michel. For a
whole week the battle raged in Paris, with in-
cendiarism and the massacre of hostages on one
side and with the butchery of suspects, including
women and children, on the other. Peaceable
citizens (of whom there were many; civil wars
are always fought by small minorities) saw sights
that could never be forgotten—hostages, including the Archbishop of Paris, being led out to
execution by the Communards, blood flowing
beneath the gates of the barracks where the
Versaillais were holding drumhead courts-martial,
Breton soldiers smashing the skulls of civilians
against the pavement with the butt of their rifles,
long files of prisoners, 35,000 in all, being marched

39

along the roads to concentration camps at Versailles which many of them would never reach. By May 28th, when the fort of Vincennes fell and the Commune was no more, the depths of horror had been plumbed. Even the London *Times*, a paper naturally sympathetic to Thiers, was shocked: " The laws of war ! They are mild compared with the inhuman laws of revenge under which the Versailles troops have been shooting, bayoneting, ripping up prisoners, women and children during the last six days. So far as we can recollect, there is nothing like it in history. . . . The wholesale executions inflicted by the Versailles soldiery, the triumph, the glee, the ribaldry of the ' Party of Order ' sickens the soul." Statistics can give no idea of the horror, but it is worth noting that the carnage was worse than the Germans had caused in any battle, and far worse than the Terror of 1793–94. The Terror had cost the lives of 2,596 people in Paris during fifteen months, but 20,000 Communards and suspects were killed in Paris in the course of that one May week. And even that was not the end: the pursuit of the Communards went on all summer till the number of arrests reached 140,000 and the courts were reducing justice to a mockery by sentencing even children under sixteen to deportation. There is truth in the remark of Rochefort's collaborator, Henri Maret: " The massacre was not only a crime; it was for the reaction a blunder. The Commune, which would

40

have faded out in ridicule, assumed a tragic grandeur."

If Clemenceau had not been turned back at the Porte St. Denis he would surely have been shot, either by Thiers' men or by the Communards. It is said that the latter arrested a swarthy young man whom they took to be Clemenceau, and were on the point of executing him when the Brazilian Consul arrived on the scene and proved that he was an unoffending Portuguese-speaking citizen of Brazil. As it was, Clemenceau made his way home to the Vendée and lived quietly with his family for a month or two. He was outwardly calm but inwardly tormented. The peace terms which Thiers had negotiated with Bismarck, and which were finally signed in the Treaty of Frankfurt on May 10th, were worse than he had feared: Germany annexed Alsace and most of Lorraine and saddled France with an indemnity of 5,000 million francs, reserving the right to keep an army of occupation on French soil until it should be paid. Clemenceau could never accept this mutilation and humiliation of his country. And the reports of the civil-war fighting and its aftermath meant more to him than to most men; he had seen what blood-lust could be, up on the Butte on March 18th.

What had happened to France, to the Frenchmen, who, in spite of the journalists' squabbles and disputes about the Constitution, had seemed so serene, so united, less than a year ago? The moral is perhaps best pointed by Félix Pécaut who, in a letter dated May 23rd, 1871, wrote of the Communards: " They lived side by side with us in the same city: we saw them every day building our houses, making our furniture, cutting our jewels, working to provide our necessities and our luxuries; but between them and us what was there in common ? What interest did we take in their private lives ? When have we ever tried to come together with them and to share with them the best of our spiritual substance, our experience of life and our knowledge, our appreciation of art and our moral ideal, all that makes life worth living ? . . . We are punishing them to-day for their attempt against social order, and there is justice in that; but we are also punishing them for our own unforeseeing egoism, for our love of a life of ease, for our forgetfulness of the necessary conditions of national and social solidarity." The problem of France henceforth would be to discover and apply these necessary conditions.

Chapter Three

The Making of a Republic

WORK—that was the programme for France after the convulsions of 1870-71: work to build up the shattered constitutions of the people; work to re-establish the little businesses, the great industries; work to pay off the five milliard francs which Bismarck's dictated peace demanded; work to build a new Constitution for the State.

Work—that was the programme for Clemenceau. He opened a surgery in Montmartre where he gave free consultations. It was a set of three rooms in the Rue des Trois Frères. An article in the *Figaro* describes them: " The first room opens off the corner of a narrow corridor; it serves as waiting-room. There would scarcely be comfortable elbow-room for five children, but more than thirty people are crammed into it, waiting their turn and pushing back those who would crowd it out still more. On the deal table and cane chairs ailing women are seated. A few men are propped against the mantelpiece, which is entirely devoid of ornament. Against each window-pane on the left is pressed a face looking out disdainfully on the late-comers crowding the courtyard and stretching in a long queue under the passage-way of the first block of buildings and out into the street. . . . Besides the door of entry are two other little doors, one on the right and the other on the left at the side of the window. The first, made of solid wood, opens into a kitchen transformed into an office; that is where Clemenceau's secretary sits. . . . The other is half wood, half glass, the panes chalked over. After three hours of waiting, we open it. We find ourselves in M. Clemenceau's consulting-room. Five pictures hung on threepence-a-roll wallpaper, an oak bureau, a mahogany arm-chair, an iron stove with its pipe climbing the wall with the aid of a dangling wire; on the windows curtains hung on string, beginning on the bottom pane and stretching exactly half-way down. That is the framework. . . . A man with close-cropped greyish hair, big black eyes, a thick black moustache, a frank and open manner, an outstretched hand, a man always correctly dressed. That is M. Clemenceau."

Medical work was not confined to the dispensary. The doctor visited the sick in their homes— " unsavoury tasks," as he said, " these errands to the worst districts of the Butte, these visits, short as they were, to the unhealthy cells of those infested hives where so many working-class families are crammed together under the fumes of decaying refuse, only quitting the germs of death in the factories for the infection of a horrible dwelling." If ever there was a social reformer in France who had reason to know what he was talking about, it was Clemenceau.

He was elected to the Municipal Council of Paris in July 1871 by voters who realized at last what part he had played during the crisis, and remembered that the first proposal for an elected Paris Council of eighty members had been made by him in March. His time was divided between his surgery and the Hôtel de Ville, where he became successively Secretary, Vice-President and President of the Council. The Council had only limited powers, for finance and the police remained in the hands of officials appointed by the Central Government, but there was much to be done, far too much for a new Council led by a young and uninfluential physician. The centre of Paris had to be rebuilt, the social services re-organized, commerce restored and, above all, the good repute of government had to be re-established in the eyes of the people. Clemenceau concentrated on this, for he knew that the success of every reform depended on it. " Let us show everyone," he said in his first Presidential address to the Council, " what can be done by application to business, by work, disinterestedness and uprightness. Let our management be above all suspicion; let us by the freedom and publicity of our discussions and our actions associate the people of the whole city with our work, so that they may exercise incessant control over their

45

representatives. By that means we shall have gained a great victory for the cause of municipal self-government, and have fulfilled once and for all the grand promise so long postponed: 'Paris for the Parisians, for the good of France and the Republic.' "

In those early 'seventies Paris led France in every industrial activity, and the French capacity for work astonished Europe. Industry and commerce revived rapidly (the war and the civil war together had lasted only ten months), loans were over-subscribed, taxes brought high yields. Clemenceau was able to tackle the problems which lay nearest to his doctor's heart—the reform of the Paris hospitals, the care of abandoned children and the improvement of the water-supply.

Work, first for the sick in Montmartre, then for Paris, then for France—that was the order of Clemenceau's effort. In February 1876 he was elected to the House of Deputies as member for Clignancourt. His reputation had not been easy to re-establish. At the trial of the assassins of Generals Lecomte and Clément Thomas he had to defend himself on a charge of culpable negligence. After the trial, a Major Poussargues, who had been captured with the generals and had narrowly escaped assassination, persisted in accusing Clemenceau of complicity. Clemenceau challenged the major to a duel and wounded him in the thigh. After this the calumnies died down,

46

but Clemenceau, like Gambetta and other anti-capitulationists of the Left, was out of national politics while the Organic Laws of the new Constitution were being framed and passed.

This Constitution of the Third Republic, which became law a year before Clemenceau was re-elected, was born in a mysterious way. It was the work of the deputies who had been elected in such haste at the moment of defeat in 1871 and who had begun their legislative career by voting for preliminaries of peace with Bismarck. They had been defeatists and they continued to be reactionaries; they could agree to the signing of Bismarck's peace and to the suppression of the Paris Commune, but they could agree on nothing else. Most of them looked forward to a restoration of monarchical rule: but under which monarch? The traditional Bourbon legitimists had a candidate in the corpulent person of the Comte de Chambord, and the followers of the Orléanist branch of the Bourbon family had the Comte de Paris, a nephew of Louis-Philippe. At one time it seemed as though these two Bourbon factions would combine. They offered the throne to the Comte de Chambord, but the old gentleman had the good sense to refuse. (The reason he gave was that he could never accept the blue-white-red flag with its democratic implication.) At the same time the Bonapartist dynasty had a more attractive candidate in Louis-Napoléon's son, and there was more popular support among the

47

French peasantry for a Bonaparte than for any Bourbon. But the supporters of dynastic rule, Legitimist, Orléanist and Bonapartist, in fact feared each other more than they feared a Republic.

Indeed, they had no longer any need to fear Republicanism, for the word had changed its meaning. It no longer stood for Red revolution; the Commune had been suppressed by Thiers acting in the name of the Republic. It no longer connoted disorder and a permanent and hopeless state of war with Germany. Thiers had established order and had restored prosperity. What is more, he had raised loans so quickly that by September 1873 the whole of the five milliard francs indemnity (£200,000,000) had been paid to Germany and the last German troops had left French soil. Republicanism was coming to mean parliamentary democracy with a strong middle-class flavour. Thiers was building up a Centre Party in the National Assembly, composed of conservative bourgeois of the type of Jules Grévy and Jules Simon, and he had succeeded in persuading Gambetta to use his vast influence outside in order to convince the lower middle-classes that Republicanism was respectable and would stand henceforth for safety first.

The aristocrats in the Assembly hoped, however, to give the word yet another meaning. They looked forward to a Republic of officers, gentlemen and clergy which would develop into something not unlike the old régime. In May 1873 they used their majority to force Thiers to resign and in November they elected Marshal MacMahon in his place as Head of the State, a safe man who could be counted on to perform his ceremonial duties with dignity and to keep the place warm for a monarchical restoration. But if MacMahon could be counted on, the electors could not. The mood of the country was veering towards the Left, and the next elections, which could not be postponed for ever, would probably return a reforming majority to parliament. The aristocrats therefore set about devising plans for a Second Chamber which would act as a check on the elected House of Deputies. Their leader, the Duc de Broglie, had an archaic scheme for a Senate of Notables in which the majority would be elderly dignitaries and nominees of MacMahon. This was rejected in favour of a Senate in which a quarter of the members would be nominated for life by the Assembly and the remainder elected for a period of nine years by a system of indirect election carefully calculated to over-represent the rural areas where the influence of the gentry was preponderant. (Each département, or county, was to be represented by two senators. The electoral colleges consisted of the deputies and county-councillors of the département, the councillors of the arrondissements and an equal number of delegates from each canton, whether it be a populous town or a hamlet.)

49

Nothing could prevent the Chamber of Deputies from being the main organ of the new French State. Directly elected for a period of four years by manhood-suffrage in single-member constituencies, the Chamber would have all the power of the British House of Commons. But the Constitution-makers were determined that the Senate should have more power than the British House of Lords. Not only was the assent of the Senate necessary before any Bill could become law, but the Senate could address the Chamber of Deputies (and vice versa) and Senators had equal rights with Deputies in the election of MacMahon's successors to the Presidency of the Republic. The Monarchists in the Assembly set great store by the office of President and managed to get three rights written in to the law establishing the office: the President was given the power to sign treaties which would be binding on France if countersigned by a single Minister, the power to dissolve the Chamber if the Senate should give its assent and the power to select the man who was to form a Ministry— though that power would, of course, be circumscribed by the need to choose one who would have the confidence of both Senate and Chamber of Deputies. An amendment to the presidential law proposing that " The President of the Republic is elected by a plurality of the votes cast by the Senate and the Chamber of Deputies united in a National Assembly " was carried by

50

one vote on January 30th, 1875. Once it was passed, the rest of the fundamental laws were rushed through by a tired and dispirited Assembly, and the Third Republic was born. The French people, remembering how many written Constitutions had been torn up in the last eighty years, did not expect it to last long. Certainly it was the least logical and least detailed of French instruments of government. There was no prefatory Declaration of Rights, no provision for solving a deadlock between Senate and Chamber, and no reorganization of local government or of the Civil Service or of the judiciary, which remained much as they had been after Napoleon's reforms. It was a hotch-potch of Monarchism, Bonapartism and democratic Republicanism, and as such it might lead to anything or nothing.

Like all good compromises, the Constitution of 1875 held out hope for every side. The monarchists expected it to pave the way to a restoration, via MacMahon's Presidency, which was due to end in 1880. The Radicals, as the men round Gambetta came to be called, hoped that it would lead to a Left régime supported by a united Republican Party. Both were quickly disillusioned. MacMahon proved to be as stupid as he was dignified. He adjourned the newly elected House of Deputies on May 16th, 1877, and called in the Duc de Broglie as Prime Minister, for no better reason than that he was afraid of a ministry led by Gambetta, now the most outstanding statesman in France. When 363 deputies presented a petition of protest, MacMahon coolly dissolved the House and attempted the grossest manipulation of the forthcoming elections. The Marshal-President had neither the prestige nor the skill necessary for such a *coup*. The result was not only a Left victory at the polls but the final discrediting of the Presidential weapon of dissolution, which no President was ever to dare to use again. MacMahon had no alternative but to resign, though he succeeded in postponing the evil day until January 1879.

At the same time Gambetta's project for a united Republican Party came to nothing, for the deputies were in no mood to accept party discipline, particularly when this meant taking orders from the incalculable Gambetta. The way was thus left open for the moderate Republicans, known as Opportunists because they promised reforms " when the time was opportune "—a phrase which Rochefort said was " parliamentary jargon meaning *never*." Their candidate, the aged Grévy, succeeded MacMahon as President of the Republic and their leaders followed each other as Presidents of the Council (Prime Ministers). Gambetta himself turned Opportunist and accepted the position of President of the House (a cross between Speaker and Leader) in 1880, greatly to the disgust of Clemenceau.

On his return to national politics Clemenceau

was a typical Radical of the extreme Left. He had opposed the peace with Germany and he had opposed Thiers. He had denied the right of the National Assembly to impose a Constitution on France since it had received no " mandate " from the electorate to do any such thing, and he had demanded the election of a special Constituent Assembly for that purpose. He had begun to distrust Gambetta from the moment when that great leader had turned to a policy of moderation and conciliation, and his distrust increased when Gambetta accepted the constituent powers of the National Assembly and agreed to the institution of a Senate. What Clemenceau wanted was a Constitution which would give all power to a single popularly elected House of Representatives, with no Senate and no effective President, a House which would use its power to destroy the economic power of the money magnates and the political power of the clergy, and to build up a strong France against the day when French rights against Germany— *La Revanche*—could be vindicated.

Most members of the Opportunist Governments would have agreed with Clemenceau in principle, but they were surely right in insisting that the time was not opportune. A too open attack on the Church would probably have driven the Catholics of France—still the majority of the population—into open opposition to the Republic. A general attack on the money-bags

53

would have destroyed the seed-grain of the French economic revival. And a too obvious concentration on military preparations would have been asking for trouble from Bismarck. They wisely preferred a policy of gradualism, knowing that France was too tired and too deeply divided for thorough-going reform. But gradualism was a difficult policy to pursue on parliamentary ground against reactionaries who refused to yield an inch and against Radicals who insisted on taking an ell. The Opportunists could never be sure of a working majority. If they were to stay in office they must have additional support either from the Right or from the Left. To rely on the Right was out of the question since the monarchists denied the whole basis of parliamentary democracy. The Opportunists therefore had no alternative but to make grudging concessions to the Left.

This put Clemenceau in a very strong tactical position. From the day when, immediately after his return to Parliament in 1876, he had proposed an amnesty for the political prisoners of the Commune, he was undisputed leader of the Radicals. A point in French parliamentary procedure gave him opportunity to use his strength. Every deputy or senator was entitled to make an *interpellation*—to demand from a member of the Government an explanation of any particular action or a statement of general policy. No procedure could have been better designed to suit a private member of Clemenceau's temperament. He had a genius for destructive criticism and had developed a highly individual debating style, stabbing at his opponents in short caustic sentences or conversing with the deputies in the intimate personal manner of the British House of Commons instead of orating at them in the tradition of French Parliaments. Against this the Opportunist Ministers with their resounding platitudes about Republican principles were highly vulnerable. They found themselves put into the dock rather than into the witness-box by Clemenceau's endless interpellations, and they lacked the weapon possessed by British Governments who could appeal to the electorate over the heads of Parliament by dissolving the House. They had therefore to get on, or get out.

The first problem was to determine the relation between Church and State. No country in which Catholics were preponderant had ever yet become a democracy. In the view of the Holy See, and therefore of the clergy, democracy and liberalism were anathema. The ideal of Republicanism, which Clemenceau once described as " the lay religion of the Rights of Man," seemed at that time to be diametrically opposed to the social philosophy of Catholicism. Republican Ministers of the Opportunist Governments would no doubt have liked to make a frontal attack on the Church, but the most they dared attempt was a sortie, and for this they chose the field of educa-

tion. The orthodox Republican doctrine was
that popular education should exclude religion
and should be in the hands of lay teachers
trained in State schools and faculties. Against
this the Church claimed the right to educate
children in the faith under teachers who had
passed through Church schools and seminaries.
The leaders of the Church in France, clerical and
lay, were monarchist or at least anti-democratic,
but they had support from many middle-class
Republican parents who preferred Church schools
and convents for their children, and among the
masses where a movement of religious revivalism
might easily be canalized into political channels.
After the Prussian war a cult of the Sacred Heart
had spread in France, symbolized by a gigantic
Church which was beginning to raise its white
domes on the Butte of Montmartre. The church
of the Sacré Cœur was built largely by money
voluntarily subscribed by the faithful, and the
Church's unparalleled faculty for tapping the
pockets of the people seemed an ill omen to
Republican Governments.

Their problem was how, without antagonizing
the mass of the faithful, to prevent the Church
from capturing the social movement and shaping
the mind of the rising generation. It was
tackled by Jules Ferry, the most judicious and
strong-minded of the Opportunists, in a Bill of
1879. His aim was to abolish the right of the
clergy to teach outside priests' seminaries, but he

wisely began with an attack on the Jesuits, who were already under a legal ban which had not been enforced, and who, as the most effective of the teaching Orders, were not popular among their fellow priests. By Article Seven of Ferry's Education Bill, " No one is to be allowed to teach in State or private schools, nor to direct a teaching establishment of any kind, if he belongs to an unauthorized religious Order." The Bill passed the House of Deputies but was rejected by the Senate. Ferry succeeded in getting the Society of Jesus banned and their schools closed, but not until 1886 were members of religious Orders forbidden to teach in State schools, and even then their right to teach in private schools remained.

Clemenceau was disgusted. As a good son of his father (who had said, " There is only one thing worse than a bad priest and that is a good priest ") he would have had the Church disestablished and separated from the State. His views on clerical influence in education remained as they had been in 1870 when he had issued a circular to all the teachers in Montmartre: " I hear that your parish priest has summoned you for to-morrow, Tuesday, to assist at High Mass with your pupils in his church. In the first place I must remind you that, being a civil institution, you are not bound by the orders of your parish priest. It is imperative that every person's liberty of conscience be scrupulously respected.

57

In summoning the children of your school to proceed in a body to any place whatever given over to the practice of any creed whatever, without consulting their individual consciences or those of their parents, you would be bringing or seeming to bring a regrettable pressure on their consciences. It is the Municipality's duty to put an end to those abuses. Like every other citizen, you are absolutely free to practise whatever religion you may choose and in whatever way you choose. Your individual pupils have the same absolute right to go to such church as they wish, with or without their parents, so long as the latter consider it suitable. But it is impossible that you should ever think of convoking them in a body to celebrate any religious rite. . . . You will observe that you are forbidden to take the children in your school to catechism. The children are free to go to catechism or not, with their parents' consent, during the holidays. But I cannot allow you to devote the time belonging to instruction to the dogmas of any religion whatever."

The quarrel over Catholic teaching did not, however, prevent progress from being made in the educational field. Under Ferry's administration attendance at elementary schools was made really free as well as obligatory, the cost being borne by local government bodies with help from the State. Important provision was made for the proper education of teachers: training colleges

58

(Écoles Normales) were set up in each département and central colleges in the Paris region for the training of lecturers and secondary-school teachers. Girls' secondary schools were planned on a national scale, and the new École Normale Supérieure for women teachers was staffed by some of the most eminent professors in the land. Emile Bourgeois was not exaggerating when he wrote in his *History of Modern France:* " In these six years (1879-85) an effort was made such as France had never seen before, an impulse which in following years resulted in the complete instruction of the children of this democracy on methodical lines."

The other major problem facing the new Republic concerned Colonies. France had once had a great Empire in India and North America but had lost it to the English in the eighteenth century; by 1815 she had nothing left but a few islands and trading stations, and by 1870 she had added little beyond Algeria and a foothold in Cochin China. Jules Ferry was determined on a policy of colonial expansion. His reasons were sound, if not sufficient. Politically, colonies would draw attention and energies away from Germany and dangerous thoughts of *Revanche*; psychologically, they would provide compensation for the humiliation of defeat; economically, they would produce raw materials and markets for the new French industries. Ferry realized that he would have to go carefully. The deputies

59

were not inclined to vote large sums of money for overseas expeditions, and the people, who in 1872 had so docilely and patriotically accepted conscription on a lottery basis for as much as five years' service in the armed forces, had no desire to send their sons to die in colonial wars.

Accordingly Ferry set about the penetration of Tunisia in 1881 by promising the Chamber that " the Government of the Republic does not seek conquests." Three months later, when Tunisia had been brought under French control and the Chamber was asked to endorse the conquest, Clemenceau launched a biting attack. Ferry had broken his promise: he had thrown Italy into the arms of Germany; he had poured away French blood in the interests of a gang of financiers whose agent was the despicable Roustan, French consul in Tunis. " I see no signs here of the institution of vast outlets for our commerce, nor of the creation of markets and of industrial undertakings; I see, in a word, nothing resembling legitimate exploitation in Tunisia. I see only men in Paris who want to do business and win money on the Bourse."

These blows told, and Ferry was forced to resign. But in the next year another Opportunist Premier, Freycinet, was carrying on a similar imperialist policy in Egypt. His case was that Frenchmen had designed, opened and in part financed the Suez Canal; the benefits would be altogether lost to France unless the French could join the British in forcing the Egyptian Government to pay interest on their foreign loans. When a nationalist movement arose in Egypt under Arabi Pasha, Freycinet sent the French fleet to join the British in suppressing it. Again Clemenceau attacked the imperialist policy, this time on rather different grounds. " Either we are going to pull the chestnuts out of the fire for the English, as in the Crimea and in China—by which we have the peril and England the profit; or else there will be a conflict between the French and the English, who in that case would be sure of German support. . . . And why should we impose on the Egyptians a government which they abhor ? "

Freycinet fell, but before long Ferry was back in power. His aim now was Indo-China, where the vast Annamite Empire, once civilized by the Chinese but never fully controlled by them, offered for French enterprise a field unequalled even by Egypt. Ferry's method was to make an excuse of the capture and death of French adventurers in order to send avenging expeditions, and then to ask the deputies to vote money, the refusal of which would involve France in humiliation. This policy he applied with such skill that for two years France waged against China an undeclared war which brought Annam and Cambodia under French " protection." But it was costly in blood and money, and the Chamber became increasingly restive. On March 28th,

1885, Ferry assured the deputies that the fighting round Lang-Son was going well. Clemenceau was openly sceptical. " The question is," he declared, " whether you, a Republican House, are going to give your electors the right to say to you: ' We elected you to make peace and you made war; you have hidden the truth from us; you have deceived us; you have betrayed your mandate; you have compromised the interests of France and the Republic.' " On the following day news of the French withdrawal at Lang-Son reached Paris. Public opinion was now with Clemenceau in wanting Ferry's blood. The Prime Minister had to face a House of infuriated and howling deputies. Clemenceau rose to his full stature in a slashing, contemptuous attack: " I will not reply to the Prime Minister. . . . All debate is over between us. . . . We can no longer discuss the interests of the nation with you. . . . The men I have before me are no longer ministers; they are men accused of high treason, and on them, if there is any principle of responsibility or of justice left, will fall without delay the hand of the law."

Ferry fell, this time finally. But the outcome was not what Clemenceau would have wished. Opportunist ministers, none of them as able or even as honourable as Ferry, were to succeed each other in power for another decade. Colonial expansion was to go on—in Madagascar and Equatorial Africa as well as in the Far East—but always with insufficient capital because Parliament was reluctant. Thus the worst was made of both worlds, for the French had to bear the cost of conquest without reaping the benefits of colonial development, while the natives got most of the kicks and few of the ha'pence of industrial civilization.

Clemenceau's case against Imperialism was based primarily on the belief that it would bring France into conflict with Great Britain; secondly, on the assumption that it would divert French energies from the task of building up the mother country. In either case, it would be playing Bismarck's game. " Why, why should we adventure 500 millions in far-away expeditions when we have our own industrial equipment to create, when we are short of schools, when we lack country roads ? If we are to rebuild France, we must not spill our blood and treasure in useless enterprises." To these arguments he added a more humane consideration: " There are much higher reasons than these for abstaining from wars of depredation. It is all an abuse, pure and simple, of the power which scientific civilization has over primitive civilization, to expropriate human beings, to torture them, to wring out every ounce of force that is in them, for the benefit of the self-styled civilizer." The hypocrisy of it all revolted him: " One begins with the missionaries, follows up with the soldiers and ends with the bankers."

It may seem surprising that so ardent a patriot as Clemenceau should not have recognized that colonies would mean a gain for France both in economic resources and in man-power. But at that time colonial development cost more soldiers than it stood to win, and the markets that were being opened seemed to mean money for speculators rather than wealth for France. At any rate Clemenceau never repented of his anti-colonial policy. Shortly before his death he told his ex-secretary, Jean Martet : " I blamed Ferry for making those colonial enterprises—I also blamed him for the way in which he made them. You can have no idea of the stupidity, the incompetence which ruled those undertakings . . . the people and the millions they gambled with, without knowing where or against whom—and all the corrupt dealing that went on behind it. A colonial policy is a good thing, Martet, when it discovers a few genuine truths for export to the poor devils, black and yellow, who otherwise wouldn't care a hang most of the time. But when it merely serves to enrich a few individuals, to found companies, to exploit capital and resources, in order to make those same yellow and black folk sweat gold, then, with your permission, it doesn't arouse much enthusiasm in my breast."

By the mid-1880's the Republic which no one had expected to last was settling down into a mould which no one had expected it to take. Nothing was left of the Republic of Notables forecast by the Duc de Broglie. The Princes of the blood had been expelled from France. In the Ministries and in the Presidential palace, where the term of the ex-lawyer Grévy had been extended, the holders of office were all bourgeois rather than men of social eminence. In the villages, where most of the population lived, the leader of opinion was the schoolmaster, usually rationalist and radical, who was beginning to usurp the moral authority previously held by squire and priest. Little was left of the Republic of Strong Government envisaged by the makers of the Constitution. The President's power of dissolving the House of Deputies had perished of misuse. The Senate had ceased, by a reform of 1884, to be an assembly of squires and elder-statesmen. The nomination of life-members was abolished and the Senate became a body of politicals elected by local government organizations. "The real beneficiaries of the reform were," in Professor Brogan's words, "the middling country towns, the homes of the doctors, lawyers, *lycée* professors who were becoming the new governing class. The Senate was no longer predominantly rural; it was now mainly a body representing the fears, the prudence, the sentiments of the petty bourgeoisie of the scores of little local capitals of around ten and twenty thousand inhabitants."

Power had fallen into the hands of elected representatives, and the deputies were motivated, to an even greater extent than the senators, by local rather than by national interests. The failure of Gambetta to build up a united Republican Party made this likely, and the failure of his Ministry of all the Talents in 1881 made it inevitable. The Ministry fell after seventy-seven days and in the following year the great man died. There was now no statesman left with the prestige and the fire needed to fuse particularist interests into support of a strong government. Gambetta had wanted to abolish the system of single-member constituencies (*scrutin d'arrondissement*) in favour of one of group-candidatures on a party-list (*scrutin de liste*), a reform which he believed would focus voters' attention on national issues. The Parliament which had refused the reform during Gambetta's lifetime passed it soon after his death, but a few years later France reverted to the single-constituency system. Deputies and senators were elected or rejected according to their promise of benefits for their particular constituents. Since local government had been left largely unreformed and local administrators, judges and even teachers were nominated by the central Departments in Paris, there was no way in which the people could have a say in the selection or a check on the behaviour of officials except by exerting pressure at the centre through their elected representatives. These gentlemen, most of whom depended on their parliamentary salaries for the greater part of their income, were besieged with requests to use their influence on Ministers for jobs, privileges and grants. The prevailing mood of France was *Enrichissez-vous,* and the deputies were not loath to help themselves while helping their constituents.

For all this, Clemenceau had a large share of responsibility. He was the arch-enemy of priest and squire and Notable, the arch-opponent of strong government, whether under Thiers or Gambetta or Ferry. His whole action had been towards strengthening the power of the legislature at the expense of the executive. He opposed the *scrutin de liste* and upheld the system of single-member constituencies, for all the encouragement it gave to the parochialism of deputies. Yet he deplored the mood of *Enrichissez-vous* and believed that France must have a strong government—if only it could be a government which he would be able to control.

Chapter Four

The Second Crisis : Panama

AFTER ten years in the Chamber, Clemenceau was at the very centre of Parliamentary
intrigue. The position did not suit him: he was
no spider but, as Allain-Targé said, a tiger, better
equipped for tearing down Ministries than for
weaving the elaborate webs on which representative government depends, better endowed
for attacking from the outside than for working
constructively from within. As an inspirer of
destructive articles in his paper *La Justice*, as a
maker of disruptive twenty-minute speeches in
the Chamber, he was unsurpassed; but he had
neither the patience and flair necessary in a
power-behind-the-throne, nor the popularity
needed in a ruler. When President Grévy invited him to form a Ministry, in 1886, he refused,
knowing that he could not command a majority
in the Senate. At the same time he knew that
no one could hold a majority in the Chamber in
face of his opposition. Freycinet, " the white
mouse," in office for the third time, also realized
that; and when Clemenceau demanded that he
should appoint a young general, Boulanger, as
Minister of War, he dared not refuse.

68

Boulanger had been Clemenceau's senior by four years at the Lycée de Nantes. He was a handsome, dashing, romantic creature, just the man in Clemenceau's view to restore the prestige of the French Army, which must be a necessary prelude to restoring the prestige of France in Europe. As Minister of War he endeared himself immediately to the soldiers by improving their clothing, rations and arms (he gave them the Lebel rifle), and to the civilian masses by holding scintillating military reviews and cutting a fine figure on horseback. When Bismarck publicly referred to him as a danger to the peace of Europe, his popularity in France knew no bounds; and when his brusque handling of an affair concerning the seizure by Germans of a French frontier agent, Schnaebele, ended in Bismarck's climbing down, Clemenceau was delighted with his protégé. The Republic might yet make France strong and respected in Europe.

But what was to make it respectable in France? Certainly not the President. An ugly scandal came to light in the presidential palace, showing that Grévy's own son-in-law, Daniel Wilson, had been selling honours and decorations. Clemenceau leapt in and forced Grévy to resign. If he had looked before he leaped, he would have realized the difficulty of finding a suitable successor to Grévy. The obvious man for the Presidency was Jules Ferry, but Ferry was Clemenceau's *bête noire*. The other candidates were all null in prestige and void of political intelligence. "I shall vote for the stupidest," Clemenceau is reported to have said, and he intrigued so successfully that Parliament elected the almost unknown Carnot.

The French people felt obscurely that they had been cheated. It had been possible to admire MacMahon, who was after all a Marshal of France, and to respect M. Grévy, if only for what he had said in 1848, but no one could feel enthusiasm for President Sadi Carnot. In their need for a figure-head the masses began to turn to General Boulanger. *Voilà un homme!* He had been a wonderful Minister of War until July 1887, when Rouvier had formed a Ministry to exclude him and had packed him off to an obscure command at Clermont. Then the Paris crowd, seeing him as a martyr to political intrigue, had made a great demonstration at the Gare de Lyon, where they tried to prevent his train from leaving for Clermont. Now they wondered why their *brave Général* was not in Carnot's place.

Boulanger for his part was not deaf to the siren voices. He was as volatile as he was dashing, as ambitious as he was vain. Soon he was flirting not only with the hero-worshipping masses and with the apostle of immediate *Revanche*, Paul Déroulède, and his League of Patriots, but also with the Bourbon and Bonapartist Pretenders. In aristocratic salons he met anti-Republicans

70

who had no difficulty in putting up money for his campaign. Under the French electoral system there was nothing to prevent a man from standing for several constituencies at the same time. The plan engineered by a certain Count Dillon, an Irish-Frenchman who had been a company promoter in the United States, was that Boulanger should present himself at every by-election that came up, until he had acquired so much publicity and so many votes in widespread areas that he would be irresistible.

The plan worked marvellously. There was some truth in what Maurice Barrès wrote in a famous novel: " Royalists saw in Boulanger their King; Republicans, their Republic; imperialists, their Cæsar; patriots saw the return of Metz and Strasbourg; peaceable people saw order; and all the restless saw an adventure which would solve all their problems." Within a fortnight Boulanger contested four by-elections: he got 12,000 votes in the Bouches-du-Rhône, 45,000 in Aisne, 8,500 in the Aube, 59,000 in Dordogne. At this point the Government made an absurd blunder. Intending to punish Boulanger, they put him on the retired list; they forgot that, while as a serving officer he was debarred from membership of the Chamber, his retirement would make him eligible. After a fifth by-election on April 15th, 1888, when no fewer than 127,000 votes were cast for him in the Nord, Boulanger entered the Chamber in triumph as deputy for the most industrialized

71

district in France and as head of the significantly named National Party.

Clemenceau had realized after the Gare de Lyon scene of July 1887 that he had backed a dangerous horse. Boulanger's programme, if it could be called a programme, was the dissolution of the Chamber and the revision of the Constitution. He was exploiting the popular impatience with politicians and the desire for a strong man. Luckily strong men, especially if they are generals, are apt to look slightly ridiculous on a parliamentary bench. Boulanger was much less formidable inside the Chamber than outside. Clemenceau left the necessary attack on him to Floquet, an old Radical hand. High words were followed by a duel with rapiers between Boulanger and Floquet, in which Clemenceau was Floquet's second. The outcome must have exceeded his wildest dreams, for the General flung himself against the myopic lawyer's outstretched rapier and wounded himself seriously in the neck. If ridicule can kill, Boulanger's ambitions would have been dead.

But again Clemenceau miscalculated. Exceptionally for France, ridicule did not kill. When Boulanger rose from his bed he still was himself as chosen leader of the ardent patriots and well-financed aristocrats as well as of the working-class people whose fathers had carried Louis-Napoléon to power by an overwhelming popular vote. In order to try out the extent of his support

72

Boulanger stood as parliamentary candidate for the Paris division in a by-election on January 27th, 1889. Nothing that Clemenceau could do could prevent the return of Boulanger by 244,000 votes, a majority of 66,000 over the other candidates combined.

Now was the opportunity for the overthrow of the Third Republic. All that Boulanger had to do, as Déroulède pointed out, was to march that very night to the Palais-Bourbon with the Paris mob behind him and to force the dissolution of the Chamber; if that failed, the mob would install him in the presidential palace. But Boulanger, for all his swagger, was no gambler. He hesitated, and the moment passed. After the night of January 27th, enthusiasm began to wane. Parliament acted quickly, passing Clemenceau's old Bill for a *scrutin d'arrondissement* which would prevent future Boulangist electoral successes in group-constituencies, banning multiple candidatures and setting up the High Court of the Senate to try Boulanger for conspiracy against the State. Boulanger was induced to leave the country—on April 1st. From that day his cause was irretrievably lost. Two and a half years later, a forgotten man, he committed suicide on the grave of his mistress in Brussels, thus, in Clemenceau's cruel words," dying as he had lived, like a subaltern."

No one will ever know how near to ruin the Republic had been in 1889. Had the Boulangist coup misfired merely because of the unstable

character of the General, or because of the dis-
unity of the forces behind him? Or had the
movement been nothing but the ephemeral effer-
vescence of the public's desire for sensation?
Only one thing was certain: discontent was widespread, and if parliamentary government was to
survive, the parliamentarians must do something
to retrieve their own prestige and that of the
Third Republic.

Perhaps it was with this in mind that Opportunist and Radical politicians entered into a conspiracy to deceive the public about the finances of the
Panama Company. The most highly respected
figure in France was Ferdinand de Lesseps, the
grand old man who had created the Suez Canal
and had launched a similar plan for the American
isthmus. The Panama Canal was to bring glory
to the Republic; on no account could the venture
be allowed to fail. When de Lesseps' plan mis-
carried and the original capital was swallowed up
in the malarial swamps of the isthmus, every effort
was made to hush up the failure and to induce
the public to take up new shares. Hushing up
meant buying the silence of anyone who professed
to be in-the-know; inducing public confidence
meant paying journalists and politicians to write
and tell fairy-stories about conditions in Panama.
This unsavoury work was undertaken with zest
and skill by Baron Jacques de Reinach, who had
influence in Opportunist circles through his
nephew and son-in-law, Joseph de Reinach, an

eminent Republican statesman. He worked so well that in 1888 the Chamber and Senate passed a Bill allowing the Panama Company to float a colossal new loan for 600,000,000 francs.

Yet somehow suspicion had arisen. Only a third of the new shares were subscribed. The Panama Company had to be wound up; 830,000 French investors lost money. The Chamber could not refuse to demand an official inquiry, though it hoped that the Government would not show any excessive zeal in carrying it out. The conspiracy of silence was observed until early in 1892, but then the truth about the Panama scandal began to leak out in every gutter of Paris.

Eventually, no doubt, leakage was inevitable— far too many people had been involved in the conspiracy; but the flood was precipitated by a quarrel among thieves. Baron de Reinach had employed in his campaigns of bribery and corruption another German-Jew of even shadier antecedents. Cornelius Hertz had been born in Besançon and had made his way to America, where he became a United States citizen and obtained a doctor's degree in Chicago before returning to France with a small fortune. Hertz had some hold over Reinach, and began blackmailing him. Cornered, Reinach tried to save himself by supplying facts about parliamentary corruption to a Boulangist journal, on condition that his own name should be kept out of it and the hue-and-cry directed to other quarters. Hertz retaliated

75

by giving new twists to his blackmailing screw until, on November 19th, 1892, Reinach committed suicide.

Now there was no stopping the spate of rumour and denunciation. Drumont made the running in an anti-Semite campaign in *La Libre Parole*, a scurrilous rag the sales of which increased every week. Déroulède surpassed him in an anti-foreigner campaign, making the most of the facts that both Reinach and Hertz were of German origin and that Hertz had sought refuge in Bournemouth, whence the British Government refused to extradite him. More dangerous still, Delahaye was taking up the case in the Chamber. This Boulangist deputy claimed to have the stubs of a cheque-book proving that a hundred and fifty deputies had been taking bribes from Reinach and Hertz. He demanded that they should all be put on trial for fraud.

The Opportunists were in an impossible position. They knew that the motive of the agitation was nothing more nor less than a desire to over-throw parliamentary government, but they could not fail to see that in the Panama scandal the Boulangists had a much more effective weapon than they had ever had in the General. Loubet's ministry fell. Rouvier's ministry fell. Rouvier's successor, Floquet, felt obliged to throw some victims to the wolves: he repealed the immunity from arrest in the case of five deputies, including Rouvier who admitted that he had taken some money " for the honour of the Republic." But even the offer to put ex-members of the Government as well as directors of the Panama Company on trial could not assuage the indignation of the Chamber. This indignation was all the more formidable for being largely assumed. The more some of the deputies felt themselves to be incriminated, the louder they shouted for a scapegoat. Cornelius Hertz had been behind the corruption, but who had been behind Cornelius Hertz ? Who had got him the rank of Grand Officer in the Legion of Honour ? Who had taken money from him for financing a journal ? Who had been with him on the very night of Reinach's death ?

" You all know," thundered Déroulède in the Chamber; " his name is on all your lips; but none of you dare say it because there are three things you fear: his sword, his pistol and his tongue. Well, I defy all three, and I name him: it is M. Clemenceau ! "

Clemenceau rose, dead white, in the silence of the Chamber. " M. Paul Déroulède," he said, " you have lied." A duel followed in which three pistol shots were exchanged. All missed, though Clemenceau had never before been known to miss unintentionally. The fear of his pistol had gone.

The deputies had their scapegoat at last. Boulangists, Conservatives and Opportunists joined in a new hue-and-cry, this time with Clemenceau as sole object. He had been bought

77

by England! He was the favourite of Queen Victoria, the tool of the Foreign Office! Were there not documents to prove it? A mulatto who called himself Norton had offered to the Boulangist paper *La Cocarde* fourteen despatches purporting to have been sent by the Foreign Office to the British Embassy in Paris, where Norton had been a servant. Among them was a memorandum stating that "Clemenceau's *alter ego*" had given the Foreign Office copies of secret correspondence between the French Government and its representatives abroad; a list of payments was appended in which £20,000 was marked to Clemenceau for the year 1893. Déroulède and his friends decided to impeach Clemenceau in the Chamber on the strength of these documents. They entrusted the case to Millevoye, whom they coached very carefully, emphasizing that his indictment must be on general grounds, and that on no account were the highly suspicious Norton papers to be produced. Fortunately for Clemenceau, Millevoye lost his head. Goaded by his victim, who was in the highest spirits and kept interrupting with almost gleeful cries of "Liar! Liar!" Millevoye read out the famous list—and the rest of his speech was drowned in the laughter of the deputies.

The Boulangists had over-reached themselves. They had thrown away the best weapon that authoritarians were ever likely to have against Parliamentary government, and in so doing they enabled the Third Republic to survive its second great crisis. Yet in the long run their agitation was not without effect. As Lord Bryce wrote in 1920, " Panama created an atmosphere of suspicion which lasted for years, like the smoke that continues to hang over the spot where a high-explosive shell has struck the ground. A scandal so tremendous seemed to confirm the vague suspicions that had existed before: and it tended to render probable charges subsequently made. . . . Nothing similar has occurred since, yet the memory of Panama has remained to be used as a reproach against Parliamentary government, even by those who knew that there were scandals in the days of Louis-Philippe, when the intellectual character of the Chamber stood high, and more numerous scandals in the eighteen years' reign of Napoleon III than the Republic has seen in the last fifty."

The immediate outcome was that Déroulède resigned, Norton and the editor of *La Cocarde* were tried, condemned and imprisoned, and Clemenceau was saved from the deputies. It had been a narrow escape. In sixteen years of parliamentary life, in the course of which he had felled no fewer than eighteen ministries, Clemenceau had made many enemies. Every Opportunist, every Conservative, every Boulangist feared and hated him, and his bitter tongue and insolent manner had left him with few close friends even among the Radicals. It was pleasant

79

as well as convenient for the deputies to divert public anger on to the Tiger. One way and another, they did very well for themselves. The Panama trials were cleverly rigged: all the accused deputies, including Rouvier, were acquitted, and only four directors of the Company and an ex-Minister of Public Works were condemned. The public bore surprisingly little ill-will against the politicians who had tried so hard to save the Panama Company "for the honour of the Republic;" if they had lined their own pockets in the process, that was only human. At the general election of August 1893 nearly all the incriminated deputies of the cheque-book were returned to Parliament. But not Clemenceau: he was thrown out with every sort of contumely by the electors in his Draguignon constituency.

When he went down to the Var for the electoral campaign, he found the constituency placarded with posters depicting him juggling with English sovereigns and singing a ditty the refrain of which was, " Aoh, yes! " Wherever he went in the Var his carriage was stoned and his lodgings besieged by crowds of peasants grotesquely intoning, " Aoh, yes! " Clemenceau realized that, apart from this absurd accusation of having sold himself to England, he would have to face two direct charges: his association with Hertz, and the general destructiveness of his parliamentary record. Much against the grain, for he had never spoken of his private life or personal ideals in public, he resolved to make a complete *apologia pro vita sua*. The occasion he chose was the eve-of-election meeting at Salernes on August 8th, 1893. Here he made the greatest speech of his life. It may be worth following in some detail, for it tells us more about Clemenceau the man than any other public utterance.

He began with typical Clemenceau irony, pointing out that it was the fortune of men of politics to be attacked: "In the old days, they were assassinated; that was the golden age. To-day, any action usually considered ignoble is thought legitimate against them: lies become truth, calumny becomes praise, treason becomes loyalty. . . .

" I have never hitherto spoken to you about myself, but now after six months of daily attacks perhaps I may be allowed for once to put myself on record. For more than thirty years I have fought for the Republic "—and he went on to recapitulate his career, beginning with the imprisonment of 1862 and then describing his work in Montmartre and as a parliamentarian and as editor of *La Justice*. This paper he had founded in 1880 with Camille Pelletan as leader-writer. " Our platform was the Republic, by the application of the ideals which have made our party: the old Republican programme—to develop the action of universal suffrage, to increase its effectiveness by the greatest possible extension of public education of every sort, to obtain a fairer incidence of taxation, to free the individual from the old monarchic chains which still bind him. With regard to the Church, liberty of conscience and the secularization of the State. In the social and economic field, the vindication of the principle which sums up the whole Republican programme —the principle of Justice. Lastly, to build the strength of defeated France, to put an end to the waste of blood and money in valueless expeditions. There is the programme which people have dared to call unpatriotic! . . . And since our first victory —that of amnesty for the men of the Commune— *La Justice* has always remembered the cause of the disinherited."

Like most honest journals of opinion, *La Justice* had never paid its way. Clemenceau admitted that one of its shareholders in the early years was Cornelius Hertz, who had put £1,000 into the paper, but this share had been bought back in April 1885 by Clemenceau himself and an announcement to that effect had been printed in *La Justice* in 1886. There remained the accusation that he had procured a step-up for Hertz in the Legion of Honour and that he had helped Hertz in his Panama machinations, getting richly recompensed for his pains. This charge, Clemenceau pointed out, was based on nothing but a simple *non sequitur*: Hertz was a spy, therefore Clemenceau must be his accomplice. No evidence had ever been adduced, except a wretched rumour that Clemenceau was rolling in money, wallowing

82

in millions of ill-gotten francs. Such rumours are not easy to refute with dignity.

" I defy anyone to find any extravagance in my way of life, beyond a saddle-horse which costs me five francs a day during nine months of the year, and a share in a shoot which comes to less than five hundred francs. Where are the millions ?

" I have settled the debts of my youth by means of a loan from a notary in Nantes. The record can be seen, for the loan has not yet been repaid. Where are the millions ?

" I gave my daughter in marriage without a dowry. Where are the millions ?

" I have lived for the last nine years in my present flat. The furniture dealer and the decorator accepted payment by instalments. I am still paying those instalments. That's the sort of admission that disinterested servants of the Republic are reduced to. Let the shame of this humiliation rest on those who made the confession necessary! "

So much for the past and the personal aspect; now for the important question, the future of the Republic:

" The whole country wants to keep the Republic. The question is to decide whether it is to be an instrument for the conservation of the old monarchical laws or for political and social reform. Nothing is more natural than that the two tendencies of the human mind—the desire to conserve and the need to change—should both be represented in the Republican ranks, and that Republicans should organize in accordance with their affinities. As I declared at Bordeaux in 1885, the Republic will not have taken definite possession of the country, will not be organized for survival and for the progress to which its destiny calls it, until it can reflect those two sentiments whose successive manifestation makes up the whole of human history."

Here Clemenceau was casting an envious eye on the English two-party system, but he knew well enough that the English system rested on a common agreement about the principles of society, whereas no such general agreement existed in France. " Instead of a conservative Republican party," he went on, " what is developing is a movement of ex-Monarchists and vacillators who take the label of the Republic in order to destroy it. Monarchism as such is dead, but what is alive—very much alive and very powerful—is the Catholic Church, the greatest organized political force in the world. . . . Sooner or later the two great groupings conjured up by history will take form spontaneously. On one side under the guidance of the Church, all the superstitions, all the vested interests, all the forces of the past—the old régime under a new flag, led into battle by the leader of the old secular beliefs. And on the other side, the vast masses of the countryside as well as of the towns— masses no longer dispersed, isolated and given up

84

to ignorance, indiscipline and to the caprices of chance, but strengthened by education, by a powerful organization, and submitting to the firm-willed leadership of men who know what they want and how to get it; who, having force and legitimacy on their side, are therefore invincible."

Now Clemenceau seemed to be launched on a Socialist oration, but it was not Socialism that he had in view, but Radicalism in the tradition of the French Revolution. "Above everything we must apply ourselves to defend and to develop the individual," he continued. "The individual is weak when isolated, often improvident or unable to assure his future, and abandoned defenceless to the domination of the State, to the bureaucracy which hedges him about in every manifestation of his activity, to the cunningly organized oppression of the firms from which he gets his hard-earned living and against which he struggles. And just because we ask that instead of being the oppressor of the weak, the State should become their defender, we find people raising the cry of State interference. Yes, of course the State can interfere to guarantee capital to big business; the State can interfere to increase artificially the price of the necessities of life; the State can interfere by putting the nation's army at the service of the employer against the striker! But no, the State which is so strong against the weak must never protect the worker in the dark factories where the causes of disease and of death pullulate.

85

Bound to the defence of the machine which has no brake, the State must look on without helping. Man may exploit man until his very life's blood is sucked out of him, and the State must stand by with a serene ' Make way for Liberty! ' . . .

" People say that we are annihilating individualism. What travesty! We protect the individual, we defend him, we develop him, we educate him. And by adding to the status of the individual, we add to the stature of the nation."

The speech which had begun as an apologia and a polemic showed signs of ending in a platitudinous peroration. Clemenceau took a grip on himself; he preferred to conclude with a lecture on party politics. " These party-fights in Parliament which people tell you are sterile, let me assure you that they are creative. If in the struggle there are some killed and wounded, they have at least the consolation of falling in a great cause. . . . These fights which seem so petty because of our personal pettiness, are grand because of the ideals which are at issue. Never condemn them: they are the life of nations. Through them nations grow, make progress. We have inherited them from the past, we will bequeath them to the future. I ask no truce in the party struggle; it is in no man's gift to grant it. . . . We must never let the detailed incidents of the fight get us down. As defenders, as victims of an ideal, we must rise to its level.

And if it is given to us to unite for one hour our aims with those of our party-opponents in a single victorious effort for the *Patrie*, then we will be blessed in our party-defeat."

A peroration, and the speech was finished. The authorities offered to arrange for Clemenceau to slip away from Salernes by the night train; he refused, and left next morning, at mid-day. By then he had lost the election. Cries of " Aoh, yes," which sped his departure from the Var, greeted him again on reaching Paris. Aoh yes! England's agent had been defeated. The traitor was out of Parliament. Parisians, by a fantastic aberration of their sense of symbolism, showed their relief by laying a wreath on the statue of Strasbourg.

It was an extraordinary ebullition of public discontent, as remarkable in its way as that which had welcomed Boulanger six years earlier. Throughout that period French parliamentary democracy had been going through a serious crisis. People felt that things were going wrong; they had no idea why. The Republic had proved a disappointment—" Ah, how beautiful the Republic was, under the Empire! " France was no longer a Great Power; the Berlin Congress of 1878 had demonstrated that Germany and England were the arbiters of Europe. Since France needed an ally, and since any approach to Germany or England was out of the question, overtures were made to the Tsar and between

87

1891 and 1893 a Franco-Russian entente was concluded. It was humiliating to find the Republic dependent on the good offices of the most reactionary autocrat in Europe, but beggars could not be choosers. The French working-classes had gained nothing by parliamentary democracy—their mood was of anger, now focusing round a multitude of Socialist and Syndicalist parties, now dispersing itself in futile anarchist outrages. The small investor had been robbed by the Panama Company, with the connivance of politicians. Something was wrong somewhere. At the root of the disease was a peculiarly rapid development of big business, involving the concentration of capital and labour in mass-manufacturing companies, in transport and traffic combines, in multiple shops, with all the social dislocation attendant on quick progress; but this diagnosis was not accepted at the time. Baffled, France wanted a strong man. Cheated of Boulanger, France wanted a scapegoat. When the Panamists succeeded in covering their tracks, no one was left but Clemenceau, the English-speaking, England-loving Clemenceau. To drive him out of public life was a great relief. Now perhaps things would go better. At any rate France was prepared to give the Republic of parliamentary democracy another chance.

For Clemenceau there could be no other chance. He realized that he had made mistakes and he recognized that he must pay for them.

88

Boulanger had been a mistake. Hertz had been a mistake; those who so much as touch pitch must be defiled, and Clemenceau had touched Hertz in more senses than one. His whole way of life had been a mistake—those supper parties at Druants, those expensive clothes and cigars, the nights at the Opera, that mistress whose previous lover had been the Duc d'Aumale, the brilliant man-about-town existence that had fitted so naturally into parliamentary and journalistic life. What had not been a mistake was the object of all his work, his political ideal, his work for Republicanism. That must go on.

Chapter Five

The Making of a Mind

CLEMENCEAU'S political career was to all appearances ended. No question of contesting another election could arise; the verdict of the Var was unequivocal. There was nothing to fall back on. His private life had gone to pieces: he had no family—his marriage was broken, his wife returned to America and his children grown up. He had few friends, and those were not in high places. Now that he had lost his salary as deputy, he had no income, only debts. At the age of fifty-two, he had to make a new start in life.

The challenge revivified Clemenceau. He was out of politics: very well, he must make a new career for himself. Somebody, probably Edmond de Goncourt, suggested writing. The idea was not immediately attractive. Clemenceau had scarcely written a paragraph for publication since his correspondence from America, and that was twenty-three years ago. As editor of *La Justice* he had left the drudgery of writing to Pelletan, Geffroy and the others. His own form of expression was the spoken word—the debating speech, the impromptu remark, the *boutade*. Writing, on

90

the other hand, was a serious business. It demanded meditation, and Clemenceau had never meditated. It was a craft, requiring an apprenticeship, and Clemenceau had served no regular apprenticeship except in medicine. It was an art, and no one had ever suggested that Clemenceau had it in him to be an artist. Again, writing was a solitary business, and Clemenceau had seemed incapable of being alone. He had lived his whole life in company; he had worked, so far as he had worked at all, in a crowded consulting-room, in the arena of the Chamber or in the delectable hubbub of a newspaper office. He had always needed an interlocutor, preferably an opponent, to strike a spark from him, and the harder the opponent, the brighter the spark. Writing meant striking the spark out of oneself, or at least out of an imagined, amorphous audience.

Driven by necessity rather than by conscious inclination, Clemenceau set himself to learn to be a writer. He took a quiet ground-floor flat in the Rue Franklin, out in the Passy suburb, and gave up his *mondain* life. He began to read seriously, and to string his thoughts together, picking up the beads he had told with his father during the adolescent walks in the Vendée. Darwinism, and the whole question of evolution. . . . Those philosophical problems of science and society, on which the Greeks had come nearest to a solution (he must study Hellenic civilization). . . . Those Vendéen villagers, who surely possessed a secret of living, for someone to discover. . . . Then Paris, the fantastic contrasts of Paris—there were truths there which only a writer could express; he must think his way into Paris life below the surface-level of politics where he had splashed so lustily.

These four strands—Darwinism, Hellenism, the Vendée, Paris life—were to be the subject-matter of Clemenceau as a writer. But subject-matter is not enough; there is always the problem of manner and form. Clemenceau's style was atrocious. As soon as he was confronted with the accusing stare of blank foolscap he became congested. The sentences laboured, over-loaded with parentheses, self-consciously literary. It would not do, and Clemenceau knew that it would not do. But after a while his pen began to run more smoothly. Once he could forget that he was writing and became excited, he slipped back into his mood as a talker and the old direct style reasserted himself, the sharp-edged, cutting style. Clemenceau found himself smiling; there was something to be said for the pen after all.

By good fortune, the need to earn his daily bread provided Clemenceau with exactly the form of literary expression that suited him best. *La Justice* was reorganized, with the founder no longer in the editorial chair but relegated to the position of contributor of a daily article. Those were the spacious days of journalism when an article meant not a half-column leader or an eight-hundred-word feature, but a solid piece of three or four thousand words. This discipline, which has been the ruin of many serious writers, was a God-send to Clemenceau. It gave him no time to be self-conscious: every morning the article must be written and handed over to the printers without possibility of revision on the morrow. It made him accept the stimulus of the topical—a stimulus which was always necessary to his nature, but which he might otherwise have decided to forswear, along with his dandified clothes, the supper-parties and other habits of his politician life. In the tiny flat in the Rue Franklin—three rooms and a cramped kitchen, an *appartement de modeste fonctionnaire*—he lived to a strict regimen, rising at five, taking a turn in the minute garden, doing an hour's physical drill under the supervision of a professional instructor and then, after breakfast, sitting down to his desk with the article to be written before the printer's boy called at noon.

In 1895 Clemenceau's first literary work was published: *La Mélée sociale*, a collection of a hundred articles from *La Justice* and *La Dépêche de Toulouse*, prefaced by a long philosophical introduction. This introduction shows Clemenceau at his worst as a writer but at his most typical as a thinker. It is a piece of Huxleian agnosticism, full of cheerful acceptance of the struggle for existence. " Is it not truly prodigious that

93

humanity has needed centuries of meditation, observation and research, has needed the efforts of thought of the greatest minds, in order to arrive, surprised, after so many ages of experience, at the conclusion that *life is a struggle?*" The necessity is, he goes on, that we should valiantly accept the *mêlée sociale* which is imposed on us. "Want and suffering, since they provoke mankind to effort, are the agents of the everlasting process which leads us, by means of the eternal struggle, to liberty, to an enlarged sense of justice, to a higher conception of humanity." Here the stoic creed is infused with English philosophical radicalism and with French perfectionism of the 1848 vintage. It is the mixture as before—his father's prescription, made tart by Clemenceau's own acid humour. But the ingredients do not blend; temperamental pessimism and ideological optimism are at war in the writer. Clemenceau, who is so deeply disillusioned about men, is full of illusions about mankind: "We no longer seek our ideal in the divine. The ideal is in humanity. To improve mankind, to perfect him, to develop his action more freely in a more favourable environment, to regulate and attenuate the horrible struggle for existence by the laws of justice and peace, that is the object of human effort."

The introduction to *La Mêlée sociale* is heavy going, but some of the articles are a delight. They include polemics against the unco' guid, the unchristian rich and the clergy, and stories of poverty full of astringent pity, with the refrain: " Christian love, fraternity—what's in a name ? *Il faut l'acte.*" They include onslaughts against the pious persons who refused to do anything for unmarried mothers and their children for fear of encouraging vice, warnings against the fall of the French birth-rate, pleas for better conditions in the mines and attacks on Yves Guyot and Léon Say, the *laisser-faire* economists of the day. Opponents who wished to indict Clemenceau as an Anglophile must have found abundant evidence in *La Mêlée sociale.* " The Englishman, hedged about by his legal rights, not one jot of which will he yield, is in a continual state of defence against those who have accepted the direction of public affairs. The meanest East-end grocer, if he has the law on his side, will find his cause suddenly becoming the cause of every citizen, and none of the powers-that-be will be able to resist. . . . It is quite different with us. Debonair, easy-going, unable to realize that the cause of others is our own cause, we let things slide, and the worst politicians, on certain occasions, have been able to perpetrate whatever they liked at our expense. Sooner or later, however, revolt follows some access of governmental folly, and then the blood flows in streams. After which we fall back into the delightful state of letting ourselves live—until the next upheaval."

The best thing in this first book, perhaps the

95

only pages that show Clemenceau's capacity as a writer, is a wonderful article, *La Guillotine*, in which he is attacking capital punishment by means of a description of the execution of Emile Henry, the assassin of President Carnot. It has qualities which any contemporary writer from Daudet to Zola might have envied and stands out from the surrounding verbiage like a hunting-horn from the baying of hounds. Needless to say, it was ignored by the public and forgotten by Clemenceau himself, who was to hand over to the executioner many culprits whose crimes were less heinous than Henry's.

A second book appeared in 1896, *Le Grand Pan*, another collection of articles with another philosophical introduction. This introduction was the most ambitious thing he had attempted, a long disquisition on classical mythology, very Renanian, but, it must be confessed, very boring. The gospel of the Great God Pan is the gospel of action. " Pan commands us: we must act. Action is the first principle, action is the means, action is the end. Sustained action of each man for the profit of all, disinterested action rising above puerile vainglory and dreams of eternal rewards, rising above the despair of lost battles and of inevitable death, action evolving towards the ideal, action the unique force and supreme virtue."

It would be unfair to take Clemenceau seriously as a philosopher but for the fact that he took himself so seriously. He was a man of action trying to rationalize his impulses and refusing the Christian *rationale*. The refusal did not trouble him, but it must continue to trouble his readers. The inscription on his title-page is from Pascal: " *Le Grand Pan est mort*," but where is the answer to Pascal ? Man's life is a struggle against his environment, but what of his struggle against himself ? " The struggle for the evolution of the human being (*l'être*)," writes Clemenceau, " is the law of life, which man softens through the compensating law of help to the weak." But whence comes this compensating law ? Clemenceau does not wait for an answer. " Suffering," he goes on, " ennobled by the pride of sacrifice, the joy of action, the joy of struggling for oneself and, through the full development of oneself, for others, that is what makes life worth living, that is what makes the beauty of the effort of life, at the cost of suffering, which is the beauty of death."

Surprisingly, Clemenceau's next book was a novel, *Les Plus Forts*. The story begins in the crumbling castle in Poitou—probably drawn from Aubraie—to which the owner, Henri de Puymaufray, had returned after wasting his youth and substance at the court of Louis-Napoléon. This ruined aristocrat had fallen in love with the wife of Dominique Harlé, a vulgarian who runs a neighbouring paper-factory. After her death, Henri devotes his life to Claude Harlé, his own illegitimate daughter, a girl of twenty when the book opens. Harlé, who does not suspect the paternity, has given her a priest-plus-pleasure education and is determined to marry her into the political ruling class, employing Madame de Fourchamps, a Parisian power-addict, for the purpose. Henri struggles to keep the girl's conscience alive and is fortunate in having an ally in a romantic young friend who is in love with her. The scene shifts from Poitou to Paris, where the paper-manufacturer is in a combine with Jewish financiers and where the Fourchamps conspires to marry Claude to a careerist deputy while setting her own cap at Harlé. A tableau-vivant organized for charity brings all the characters together, and in the dénouement Claude is left pledged to a *mariage de convenance* with the careerist, and Harlé to an absurd *mariage d'amour* with the Fourchamps.

Such, baldly, is the plot. But the book is essentially a *roman à thèse*, the thesis being that the strongest (*les plus forts*) are always led by their passion for power to combine against the weak and against the weaknesses in their own nature— that is, against their better nature. The paper-manufacturer, the financiers, the deputy, the society-lady are types of *les plus forts*, in unholy alliance for power. The moral is pointed in the final paragraph where a factory-hand says to Henri de Puymaufray : " You see, the strongest, in order to be the strongest, are obliged to tear out their own hearts. They won't always be the strongest, though. The weak will have their revenge." To which Henri replies : " Before the victorious assault the moat must be filled with dead soldiers. The genius of living humanity will be built up, through suffering, with lost lives (*vies manquées*)."

Clemenceau set a great deal of store by this novel. The tone throughout is earnest, which must have been a great strain for the author, and the writing is taut in the early Poitou scenes, where there are touches of the *Médecin de Campagne*, though it drags when it comes to the Paris salons. On the whole, *Les Plus Forts* is probably as good as any novel written by a statesman, including those of Disraeli, with which it has many points of resemblance. Paris criticism, however, was not benevolent. The book was a flop. Clemenceau had to realize that he could never be a novelist.

As if to cover his failure, Clemenceau published in the same year (1898) a little volume of sketches of Jewish character, *Au Pied du Sinai*, in which he retold the fable of Midas, described the caftaned Jews at Carlsbad, contrasted the plight of their brethren in the mud of the Galician villages, dropped in a tale or two about the middle-class Jew in France, and concluded that there must be charity between races as between individuals. Clemenceau could write this sort of thing in his sleep ; the only questions were whether it was

99

worth writing and why he was content to skate on the surface of the Jewish problem.

Au Pied du Sinai was an elegant trifle ; it did not add to his reputation one way or the other. His next book, however, showed an immense improvement on all the earlier work. In *Au Fil des jours*, another collection of articles, published in 1900, the introduction is brief, the doctrines crystallized in epigrams. " One must submit to the law of life : that is the last word in human wisdom. Even the gods of Olympus were subject to Fate. . . . It is beginning to be clear that nothing has action on men except ideas. He who thinks publicly, acts." The political articles have a new bite, especially the pleas for a better treatment of convicts and conscripts ; the travelogues have a sharper flavour, particularly the notes written from Carlsbad, where he went every year to take the cure and found occasion for ridiculing all the German visitors and even a few of the English—notably a young female devotee of the " Souls." The Vendéen sketches in the first part of this volume are probably the best thing that Clemenceau ever wrote ; *Mdlle Stéphanie*, the tale of a provincial old maid who came into a fortune, is unforgettable, and *La Roulotte*, the legend of a gypsy's cart, is an almost perfect short story in the Maupassant vein. Elsewhere in *Au Fil des jours*, Clemenceau is developing not only a personal style but a form of his own. He is writing causeries rather than articles. There is less abstraction, less exhortation and a much nicer sense of satire. Anatole France could hardly have bettered *Le Banquet qui n'a pas eu lieu,* a tilt at the Franco-Russian alliance : and for the allegory of the pigeons entitled *Les Bêtes* there is no parallel.

Quotation from this last is irresistible. Clemenceau is watching the tree in his garden where his pair of white birds have been joined by a blue male pigeon. The two males fight interminably, the white prevailing only when his mate has eggs to defend. " One day, the white hen—whom I regard as hysterical to the last degree—got the idea of sitting without having taken the preliminary precaution of laying an egg. The white male took his turn in the nest where he would sit for hours, by force of suggestion contentedly covering the emptiness. I noticed that he developed the access of courage demanded by the paternal occasion and conquered the blue pigeon with as much spirit as if he really had something to defend. He had faith : that's the important thing.

" Even among birds, therefore, the strength of illusion is no less than that of reality. Falsehood or truth, one must have faith in order to be strong. Falsehood itself is a source of power. Thus does the behaviour of pigeons explain the slowness of human progress."

Pervading *Au Fil des jours* is the old disillusionment with men and generous faith in mankind.

" I have no illusions either about individuals or about the sovereign masses. I believe in pity, in the generous outburst of the spirit, in the thirst for justice in the hearts of isolated men as in the hearts of assemblies. I believe that there emerges from this state of mind, diversely according to human nature, a power of thought, a power of will and action—a single impulsion to give oneself to others. If we kill Hope, there is, as Mirabeau rightly said, only death for humanity. Well, humanity has no intention of dying yet. Our gospel must be hope in the victory of ideals which will arise from ephemeral defeat. We must preach confidence to each and all. Confidence in reason, confidence in action, confidence in fallible mankind which gropes its way towards justice."

In all this Clemenceau was preaching to himself. He needed to insist on the necessity of hope because he felt so hopeless. The cynicism and nihilism of his temperament were in conflict with the optimism and liberalism of his ideas. The outcome was a surprising vagueness whenever he set himself to write about social reform. He was a Republican, but he had no faith in the sovereignty of the people : " What is called for convenience the People," he wrote in *Le Grand Pan*, " is apparently the mobile mass of changing interests, floating on all the winds of prejudice, of atavistic dreams, of passions, of desires. Who would dare to pretend that the People rules—has ever ruled ? . . . The People is

King : it reigns, but it does not rule." He was a democrat, but he had no faith in universal suffrage. "The popular vote which has been so stupidly feared," he wrote in *Les Plus Forts*, " is the force of inertia in its present form. Our politicians have been waiting for the last twenty years for it to give an impetus. You see the result. Action, whether in practice or in thought, comes from the individual, from the man who is different from his fellows."

Throughout his writing on democracy Clemenceau was a disciple of John Stuart Mill, his first master. He was echoing Mill's fear " lest the inevitable growth of social equality and of the government of public opinion should impose on mankind an oppressive growth of uniformity in opinions and practice." He could repeat the lesson which Mill had learned from experience, that " many false opinions may be exchanged for true ones, without in the least altering the habits of mind of which false opinions are the result." Mill had denied that the " trampling, crushing, elbowing and treading on each other's heels, which form the existing type of social life," are " anything but disagreeable symptoms of one of the phases of industrial progress." Clemenceau insisted in his first book : " Let us make society profitable to all, not merely to a few. Society must be kinder to the failure, sterner to the oppressor, a severe guardian of life. It must rise to a higher conception of duty. . . . Above all, let

103

us act, since our virtue is to protest by action against the cruel stepmother Nature, against the stupid brutality of force, against successful insolence, contempt, indifference and fear. And let us spend ourselves without counting the cost." He was never more specific than this ; no programme of political action emerges from Clemenceau's social philosophy.

Prodiguons-nous sans mesure : that was Clemenceau's first commandment. He certainly spent himself as a writer. Besides the daily article in *La Justice* and occasional contributions to *La Dépêche de Toulouse* and other papers, he published five books between 1895 and 1900. He even wrote a play, *Le Voile du bonheur,* which was put on in Paris in 1901. As a creative writer he was not a success—the play, like the novel, was to be a failure—but as a commentator on the social and æsthetic world he had established himself after a few years' work in the very front rank of French *littérateurs.* Ernest Vaughan offered him a daily column in *L'Aurore,* a paper founded in 1897 with abundant capital and with Anatole France and Francis de Pressensé among its regular contributors. Hence he could reach a wider public than through the impecunious *Justice.* Whatever he might think of his failure as an artist, Clemenceau had made a success of his new career. That was some consolation to him, if not much.

If Clemenceau's first commandment was *Prodiguons-nous sans mesure,* his second was *Honour*

the æsthetic impulse in all its manifestations. He had
been an amateur of the arts in his student days
and an amateur he became again in his fifties.
Reviving his friendship with Alphonse Daudet,
he attended every Friday the meeting of writers
who later founded the Académie Goncourt. His
passion for the theatre had never left him, and
now that he was not without influence as a critic,
he helped to launch the sociological drama of
Octave Mirbeau and ranked with Jaurès among
the public men who did most to make Ibsen
popular in France. (*An Enemy of Society* was his
favourite play. How he approved Dr. Stockmann
and his closing words : " The strongest man upon
earth is he who stands most alone ! ") Music
was a new love and his appreciation was always
limited by his prejudice against anything that
came out of Germany, but the work of the new
French composers was a revelation to him and he
became the friend, and to some extent the patron,
of Debussy and Fauré. Poetry he failed to
appreciate, especially the poems of the *Symboliste*
school which was fashionable in Paris in the
'nineties ; he could see nothing but pedantry and
wilful obscurity in Mallarmé and Valéry.

Painting was his favourite among the arts and
had been ever since he had begun buying
Japanese prints which he could ill afford, back in
his prodigal thirties and even before that when,
as a student, he had seen his first Monets and had
gone out of his way to meet their author. He

responded with the enthusiasm of an adolescent
to the combination of science and sensuality in
Impressionist painting and to the massive personality of Claude Monet. Now, in their fifties,
a close friendship sprang up between the restless
ex-politician and the silent, detached painter.
" Painting," Constable used to say, " is a science
in which pictures are the experiments." The
experiments of Monet in his twenty versions of
Rouen Cathedral discovered something to
Clemenceau that was an abiding inspiration.
" With the Impressionist school the sovereignty
of light is affirmed," he wrote in *La Justice* in May
1895 (an article which was reprinted in *Le Grand
Pan*). " The eye of Monet is a pathfinder guiding
our visual evolution towards a more subtle and
penetrating vision of the world." As for the
professional critics . . . he quoted the *Figaro* on
the Exhibition of 1874—" The impression left by
the ' Impressionists ' is that of a cat walking on
the keys of a piano or of a monkey which has got
hold of a paint-box "—and the dictum of M.
Ballu, inspecteur des Beaux Arts, on Monet and
Cézanne in 1877—" The first exhibits thirty
canvases, the second fourteen. One must see
them to imagine what they are. They provoke
laughter and are altogether lamentable. They
show the most profound ignorance of design, com-
position and colour. Children amusing themselves with paper and paints can do better."
Clemenceau went on to suggest that the President

of the Republic, Félix Faure, should buy the twenty Cathedrals for the nation : " History will take count of these paintings, be sure of that ; and if you have the legitimate ambition to live in the memory of man, hold on to the coat-tails of Claude Monet, the peasant of Vernon. It is a surer method than to rely on the Versailles Congress or on the policy of ministries."

No one who confines his view to politics can understand France, much less love her. The function of France throughout history has been to provide a form, a culture, in which the various schools of the European spirit can grow. The Gothic inspiration did not come from France, but it was on French soil that the first and finest Gothic cathedrals were built. The inspiration of scholastic philosophy did not come from Frenchmen, but it was on the Mont Ste Geneviève that scholasticism lived and breathed and had its being. The fathers of the Renaissance were Italian, but France was its mother, giving the movement its Christian name and moulding its character. The progenitors of the National ideal were not Frenchmen, but France was the first firmly established National State. Even the ideas of the great Revolution came from outside France—from seventeenth-century Englishmen and from the Genevan Rousseau—but the Revolution was the French Revolution. France has been the matrix of Western civilization, the womb where the embryos gestate, the foyer where the children of the spirit are brought up. Goethe said that France is every man's second country. In a sense she is his first. Certainly she is the artist's first studio, the place where he can work best and bring his creations to fruition.

France was performing this function as fully in the eighteen-nineties as at any time in her history. The new movements in European painting and music, poetry and philosophy, physics and chemistry were all essentially French. Many of the great innovators were foreigners, but Whistler and Van Gogh, Scriabin and Wilde, Marie Sklodowska Curie and Picasso all made their homes in France. The great achievement of the Third Republic lies in the arts and sciences rather than in politics.

Just as Clemenceau had been at the centre of the movement in politics, so was he at the centre of the movement in the arts, though as an amateur rather than a professional. He induced the Ministry of Fine Arts to buy Whistler's *Portrait of the Artist's Mother* for the nation ; he wrote appreciatively of Cézanne ; he sat for Monet and for Rodin ; he got Toulouse-Lautrec to do eleven lithographs for *Au Pied du Sinai* and Fauré to compose the incidental music for *Le Voile du bonheur*. It would be too much to say that he gave an impulsion to French æsthetic life and thought as he had given an impulsion to politics. The movement gave him an impulsion, reviving his zest for life.

Yet there was something missing. It was not in Clemenceau to be an artist. He had taught himself a new trade, he had recovered his moral and physical health, he had educated himself through reflection and appreciation ; yet all this was but an apprenticeship for something else. " He who thinks publicly, acts," he had written, but he did not quite believe it. His nature demanded another sort of action, outward action, a fight against an external enemy, for a cause. By good fortune a cause was at hand in 1897 as it had been in 1870. This time it bore the strange device of Dreyfus and was to absorb all Clemenceau's energies for two hectic years.

Chapter Six

The Third Crisis : Dreyfus

THE Dreyfus affair is one of the curiosities of modern history. In appearance it was trivial—a miscarriage of justice in the case of an army captain, exposed after a lapse of years, mitigated by a new trial and ultimately set right by the pardon and reinstatement of the condemned officer. In reality it was a major moral crisis which anticipated many of the essential conflicts of the twentieth century—a *crise de conscience* which convulsed France and forced her to face the implications of her Republican creed.

The story begins in 1894 when the Ministry of War became convinced that there was a leakage of military secrets from the General Staff. The Panama affair had shown that the French Parliament and judiciary were reluctant or impotent to investigate scandals ; the Ministry of War was determined to prove that there was one institution in France that could deal effectively with corruption. At that time the Hertz-Reinach exposures were fresh in the public mind and anti-Semitism was an increasingly popular cause, thanks to the Press campaign led by Drumont in *La Libre Parole.* Nothing more natural, therefore, than that the War Ministry should pin the guilt for the leakages on Temporary Staff-Captain Alfred Dreyfus, the first and only Jew to hold a Staff appointment. Dreyfus was tried by court-martial on December 22nd, found guilty of treason and sentenced to deportation for life to Devil's Island.

Clemenceau took his guilt for granted and inveighed against the lightness of the sentence. " A man reared in the religion of the Flag, a soldier honoured with the care of secrets of national defence, has betrayed his trust ! " he wrote in *L'Aurore* on the day after the court-martial. " Certainly I want the death penalty to be erased from our legal codes. But everyone will understand that the Military Code should of necessity be its last resting place. . . . Alfred Dreyfus is a traitor, and I shall not insult any soldier by putting him in the same category with this scoundrel." This opinion was shared by all politicians, including Jaurès, who declared in the Chamber that " if Dreyfus has not been shot as a traitor, it must be because the Government would not have it, although the law permits the penalty."

For nearly three years nothing more was heard of Alfred Dreyfus. His brother Mattieu and a Jewish journalist, Bernard Lazare, did their best to keep the condemned man's memory alive, but no one took any notice ; it is natural to defend one's kin and Jews are notorious for carrying family loyalty too far. One day at the end of October 1897 Arthur Ranc came into the *Aurore* office and with a great air of solemnity told Clemenceau that Dreyfus was innocent. Clemenceau scoffed, but his expression changed when Ranc went on to insist that Scheurer-Kestner had proofs. Scheurer-Kestner, Vice-President of the Senate, was the most highly respected of all the Alsatians who had thrown in their lot with France after the partition of 1871 ; his integrity, like his patriotism, was beyond all doubt. Clemenceau reached for his hat and went round to the Senate. There Scheurer-Kestner explained the conclusion he had reached : the manuscript note (*bordereau*) on which Dreyfus had been convicted was not in his handwriting ; the court-martial had been misconducted and fresh evidence which had come to light since the trial had been suppressed ; justice demanded that there should be a retrial.

By the end of November part of the story was out. A newly appointed Chief of the Intelligence Section of the General Staff, Colonel Picquart, had discovered that the handwriting of the *bordereau* was that of a Commandant Esterhazy and that there were other documents pointing to Esterhazy's complicity with German agents. The War Ministry had rewarded Picquart for his zeal by relieving him of his post and sending him on a mission to the interior of Tunis. But before his departure to what was obviously exile, Picquart had been able to commit his evidence to his friend, the advocate Leblois, who had passed it on to Scheurer-Kestner. *Le Matin* published a facsimile of the *bordereau* with the intention of emphasizing Dreyfus's guilt, but the effect was to incriminate Esterhazy.

Clemenceau was still not convinced that Dreyfus was innocent, but he could no longer doubt that the court-martial had been irregular and that someone high up in the War Ministry was over-anxious to shield the Hungarian-born Esterhazy. He agitated in *L'Aurore* for a trial. This was held on January 9th, 1898, with the result that Esterhazy was acquitted and Picquart dismissed from the service. But the attitude of the War Ministry was highly suspicious. The Army chiefs were protesting too much, and Picquart's successor in the Intelligence Section, Colonel Henry, was openly feeding certain Paris newspapers, notably *L'Eclair* and *L'Echo de Paris*, with propaganda material in an attempt to turn attention from legal evidence into the happier hunting-ground of anti-Semitism.

Clemenceau had just reached the conclusion that something must be done, and done quickly, when Zola burst into the *Aurore* office with the manuscript of an article. It was headed " Open Letter to the President of the Republic," and in it Zola accused by name five generals and two other high-ranking officers of having engineered or connived at the irregular trial of an innocent man on false evidence. He accused the Ministry of War of having conducted a Press campaign in order to cover its mistakes and to mislead public opinion ; he accused the first court-martial of "having violated the law by condemning an accused man on evidence which was kept secret, and the second court-martial of having covered this illegality, *par ordre*, by committing in its turn the judicial error of knowingly acquitting a guilty man."

The article was obviously dynamite. Clemenceau insisted that it should be printed at once : there must be only one change, the title. He scribbled across the top the briefest of headlines— "J'ACCUSE."

On January 13th, 1898, *L'Aurore* appeared with *J'accuse*, signed by the most famous novelist of the day, in Clemenceau's usual column. The sensation was immediate and immense. Two hundred thousand copies were bought in Paris alone. Zola's article acted as a catalyst, precipitating the city into two camps, Dreyfusards and anti-Dreyfusards, revisionists clamouring for a retrial and anti-revisionists. Among the Dreyfusards were men of all parties and creeds who believed in the rights of the individual and the sanctity of justice—dignitaries of the University led by Lucien Herr and professors of the Ecole Normale, pillars of the Senate headed by Scheurer-Kestner and Trarieux, and leaders of the Chamber of Deputies ranging from Jaurès the socialist to his arch-opponent the Catholic Comte de Mun who was now demanding that the Government should act. In the other camp were the old-guard patriots who insisted that a retrial would cast a slur on the honour of the Army which must be kept immaculate at all cost ; the type of Republican who put *raison d'Etat* before the rights of the individual and who believed that a retrial would be playing into the hands of the enemies of France ; the Catholic clerics, particularly in the Jesuit and Oratorian orders, who saw in Dreyfusism nothing but a conspiracy of Protestants, Free-Masons and Jews ; the professional Jew-baiters of the Drumont stamp ; and the cabinet ministers presided over by Méline (once a colleague of Zola and Clemenceau on the under-graduate paper *Travail*) who wanted a quiet life and were anxious to let Dreyfus and all other sleeping dogs lie.

Clemenceau had taken a line of action which surprised many of the men who thought they knew him best. As Léon Daudet wrote in *La Vie orageuse de Clemenceau*: " Here was he, an out-and-out Revengist whose obsession was national defence, throwing in his lot because of this affair with those who were hostile or at any rate in-different to the very ideas which were nearest to his heart. The contradiction had taken such a hold of him that it led him to call the generals ' beplumed octopuses ' and grossly to insult one or two of them, thus forswearing for the sake of a Jew, who later turned out to be completely

uninteresting, the strongest of his convictions."
But the strongest of Clemenceau's convictions
was expressed in the title of his first paper, *La
Justice* : " The cause of human right," he said,
" is indivisible ; one must either be for or
against."

Zola's article was on the face of it a criminal
libel. In February the writer and his publisher
were put on trial, with Labori acting as counsel
for Zola and Clemenceau himself defending
L'Aurore. The court-room was packed and its
atmosphere hysterical. When Clemenceau stood
up he was greeted with shouts of " Cornelius
Hertz ! " which the judge made little effort to
quell. His speech was not so much a defence of
L'Aurore as an attack on the men who were
shielding Esterhazy and covering up a miscarriage
of justice. Towards the end he had one famous
phrase : pointing to the crucifix hanging on the
wall behind the Bench, he said : " Christ Himself
was the victim of a judicial error, yet there He is,
hung behind the judge's back, no doubt so that
they should not see Him."

Zola and the manager of *L'Aurore* were sentenced to imprisonment and a heavy fine. The
anti-Dreyfusards had won the first round. Their
victory was celebrated by a burst of anti-Semitism
led by the triumphant Drumont. Clemenceau
slashed at him in *L'Aurore* and Drumont replied
with a personal insult. The inevitable duel
followed. The conditions were that three pistol

shots should be fired by each opponent at a distance of only twenty yards. Drumont, who was shockingly short-sighted, missed each time ; so, for reasons which will never be known, did Clemenceau. In the Press battle, however, Dreyfusard shots hit the mark. The War Ministry spokesmen could not prove their contention that Dreyfus had confessed his guilt; their view of the authorship of the *bordereau* was denied by as many handwriting experts as had confirmed it ; their collateral evidence was shown to have been concocted by Colonel Henry years after the court-martial. Clemenceau in *L'Aurore* and Jaurès in *La Petite République* were scoring shot after shot on the target against the wild firing of Rochefort in *L'Intransigeant* and of Déroulède, Drumont and their supporters in the ultra-national, Catholic and anti-Semite Press. In July the new Minister of War, Cavaignac, had to come into the open to rescue the anti-Dreyfusards. He was an attractive personality with a fine reputation as Republican and man of honour. He explained to the Chamber that he had definite proofs of Dreyfus's guilt—not the *bordereau*, but three finally incriminating papers, two of them initialled with a " D " and the third signed " Dreyfus " in full.

Jaurès had lost his seat and there was no one in the Chamber to challenge Cavaignac's documents as Clemenceau had challenged Millevoye's in 1893. Cavaignac waved his papers before the deputies and the deputies voted their confidence in him *nem. con.* The anti-Dreyfusards had won the second round. But their opponents returned to the attack. If there were documents, let them be published : let the public judge if they were any more authentic than the *bordereau* ! Cavaignac tried to propitiate both sides by putting Esterhazy under arrest and by charging Picquart under the official-secrets act. This wobbling produced a new Press campaign of such vigour that Cavaignac lost his temper. He threatened to arrest the Dreyfusard leaders—the whole lot of them, from scribblers like Jaurès and Clemenceau to Scheurer-Kestner, the Senator.

At that moment the truth, which the Dreyfusards had known but could not prove, suddenly came to light. Cavaignac's own handwriting expert announced that the famous documents were a forgery and that the forger was none other than Colonel Henry himself. Henry was committed for trial and put in gaol. There he killed himself after confessing his guilt.

The Dreyfusards had won. Alfred Dreyfus was clearly innocent. But as Clemenceau was to say in after-years, " From this moment the discussion ceases to be whether or not Dreyfus is guilty but begins to turn on whether or not Jews are birds of ill-omen, whether or not it is desirable that a Jew be the guilty party, whether it is bad for the country and the Army that a court-martial may have been in error, and so forth. Arguments of that sort can just drag on till the world itself

118

comes to an end." The case against Dreyfus had
become identical in many minds with the case
against Jews, the case against lukewarm patriots,
the case against the critics and opponents of
France. Since the elections of 1898 had returned
a predominantly Dreyfusard Chamber, the patriotic struggle must be carried on outside parliament. Déroulède, who had learnt nothing by
the failure of his projected *coup d'état* of Boulanger
days, went so far as to attempt another in
February 1899. The aristocracy was in full cry
against the parliamentary Republic ; its figure-
head, the inoffensive President Loubet, was
assaulted by the Baron de Christiani at a race
meeting in June. The Chamber, thoroughly
alarmed, now demanded a change of government. Loubet called first Poincaré, then Léon
Bourgeois, to form a Ministry, but each excused
himself and the President's final choice was
Waldeck-Rousseau, one of Gambetta's young
men, who formed a strong Ministry of National
Defence.

The Government was committed to the retrial
of Dreyfus, but feeling in Paris was running so
high that it seemed wise to send the Court to sit
at Rennes. When the trial opened in August
someone shot Labori, the counsel for the defence.
The judges, if not intimidated, were timid : by
a convenient majority of five to two, they decided
in defiance of all the evidence that Dreyfus was
guilty, but, tempering the wind to the shorn

lamb, they reduced his life-sentence to ten years, five of which had already been served.

It was a fantastic decision, violating at the same time justice, logic and expediency. Anti-Drey-fusards and Dreyfusards alike were furious. The Government realized that the affair might yet lead to the overthrow of the Republic. The Prime Minister, Waldeck-Rousseau, an Opportunist and the best statesman that France had had at the helm since Jules Ferry, decided to play for safety. He got the President to declare that Dreyfus was pardoned.

Pardoned ! Clemenceau could not contain his anger. What was a pardon when justice was at stake ? Dreyfus must be exonerated by a court of law and reinstated in the Army : that was simple justice, and nothing else would suffice ! But here Clemenceau found himself opposed by his own colleagues. The Dreyfus family, now that Alfred was home and at liberty, were well content to let the matter drop. Jaurès believed that the substance of victory had been won and that it was impolitic to pursue the shadow.

In this Jaurès was undoubtedly right and Clemenceau wrong. The two-years' agitation round the name of Dreyfus had forced Frenchmen to search their consciences and to give an answer to the old question : What is meant by the Republic ? The conclusion reached by the majority was that it stood for the Rights of Man, for civil liberties, for the inviolability of law, for racial and religious toleration. Those who opposed this conception—those who stood for " my country right or wrong," those who upheld the honour of the Army against the sanctity of law, those whose habit was to regard Jews, Protestants and Free-Masons as the enemies of France—now began to appear in their true colours, as anti-Republicans. Patriots they might be, devout Catholics most of them were, but democrats they most certainly were not. The anti-Dreyfusards of that day became the authoritarians of the morrow. Charles Maurras, the young journalist who had defended Henry's forgeries on the ground that they served the cause of France, became the leader of the Royalist movement known as *l'Action Française*. Maurice Barrès, the most sensitive of the anti-Dreyfusard writers, became an open anti-Semite and apostle of the doctrine of Race. Anti-Dreyfusism lived on as an anti-democratic movement, sometimes Royalist, sometimes Catholic, but always reactionary and always—except perhaps in the moment of agony when Pétain capitulated to Hitler in 1940—in a minority. The Dreyfusards, on the other hand, had France behind them. Of this the General Elections of 1902 was the first proof. Jaurès returned to the Chamber at the head of a greatly increased Socialist party. The Radicals were even more successful : they had been Dreyfusard to a man, whereas the Marxist wing of the Socialists under Jules Guesde had taken a neutral position, holding that the Dreyfus affair was a quarrel between capitalists and therefore none of their business. The new Prime Minister, Emile Combes, was an out-and-out Radical. With a Left coalition (known as the Bloc des Gauches) behind him, he was able to set about rebuilding the Republic on the foundations laid by the Dreyfusard victory.

Clemenceau was slow in realizing that the substance of victory had been won. He had enjoyed the Dreyfus affair. It had fused the contradictory elements in his make-up—the nervous need for battle and the intellectual need for truth—as the war against the Prussians had fused them nearly thirty years before. He could no more admit that the fight had ended in victory in 1899 than that the war had ended in defeat in 1871. Not content with his effort, which that fine critic Daniel Halévy was to call " one of the great achievements of French journalism, a close-knit discussion carried on over two years, sustained each morning by an article sparkling with wit, vigour and rationality," he fought on for the rehabilitation of Dreyfus, seeing enemies everywhere. Jules Guesde, who had found tactical reasons for refusing to support Dreyfus, came in for the sharpest attacks, but he laid about him in all directions. He was touchy, impossible to work with. In December 1899 he resigned from *L'Aurore* and in the following year, finding polemical journalism as necessary to him as his daily physical jerks, he scraped together enough money to launch a little weekly, *Le Bloc*, almost every word of which he wrote himself. *Le Bloc* ran for fourteen months, carrying articles on every manner of subject from the theatre to the Chamber (which he called, after its then President, the Folies-Doumer), from the Franco-Russian alliance to the *maison de tolérance* alleged to be kept by the Jesuits in Shanghai. (It may be worth recalling that the final number was headed *Le Poincarisme*. Poincaré was characterized as " a man representative of his generation, showing a dissociation of intellect and character, a desire to be with *les plus forts*.") These articles showed no development in Clemenceau's thought. He was still living in the Dreyfus affair. He published the Dreyfusard articles in seven little volumes between 1899 and 1903. In that last year he brought out a collection of more general articles, *Aux Embusquades de la vie* ; it was no advance on *Au Fil des jours*. Writing, even polemical writing, was no substitute for action.

The electoral success of the Bloc des Gauches in 1902 brought Clemenceau back into the public eye. It was absurd that so doughty a champion of the Bloc should be out of parliament and have no other means of expression than his little weekly sheet. A change in the ownership of *L'Aurore* led to his return to the paper, this time as editor-in-chief. Then a senatorial vacancy occurred in the Var, his old constituency.

Clemenceau was approached : would he let his
name go forward ? It was a difficult decision.
He had always denounced the Senate as an
excrescence on the Republican body politic ; he
had been out of Parliament for four years and
now he was over sixty ; he had always poured
scorn on men who in their old age repudiate the
doctrines of their prime. But . . . Clemenceau
consented and was elected to the Senate as
member for the Var in April 1903.

It was the spring-tide of Radicalism in France.
The moral victory of the Dreyfusards meant something approaching a political revolution. Waldeck-Rousseau had realized this and in his
moderate way had set some reforms in motion,
making a Socialist, Millerand, Minister of Social
Affairs, putting Déroulède on trial before the
Senate, which exiled him and his leading confeder-
ates, dissolving the Assumptionists, the noisiest of
the ultramontane religious orders. Combes was
now putting into immoderate practice the very
reforms which Clemenceau had struggled for a
generation to get Opportunist Governments to
implement. From minor reforms like the abolition of censorship on plays and the removal of
exemptions from military service to major reforms like the expulsion of the monks and Jesuits,
the tide was flowing his way. In the greatest
issue of the day—that of the relation between
Church and Republic—the policy of the Combes
Government was that of the young Clemenceau.

One by one the props which upheld the power of the Church in politics, property and propaganda were being swept away. The religious Orders, men's and women's alike, contemplative as well as teaching Orders, were dissolved, all except five which were allowed to remain under strict State surveillance. The Concordat with Rome was abrogated and the Church was separated from the State, so that Catholicism ceased to be a subsidized religion and the clergy lost their official status. State-subsidized education became the business of laymen, the monopoly of the centralized *Université* controlled by a Minister of State.

Clemenceau found himself in the position of seer whose prophecies have been realized and who is not enamoured of the result. The reforms were all being made in the blessed name of liberty, but might not this liberty be a new tyranny? Might not new presbyter be old priest writ large? In a speech in December 1903 he warned the Senate: "I oppose the omnipotence of the lay state because I see in it a tyranny ; other people oppose it merely because it is not their tyranny. . . . Because I am the enemy of Kings, Emperors and Popes, I am the enemy of the omnipotent State." And he went on to criticize the Combes policy of State monopoly of education on three grounds. First, as a monopoly it might be deadly in bad hands—as in Austria-Hungary where the State had deprived the clergy only to let the clergy control the State. Second, it would drive Catholic parents into revolt and would lead them to nullify the schoolteachers' instruction by their own teaching in the home. Finally, being a monopoly, it was the negation of liberty. Clemenceau's own views on education had been set out in *Le Grand Pan* years ago. " So long as we retain the single centralized *Université* created by the Empire, so long as we refuse to set the teaching profession free from its chains, we shall deprive educational action of its strongest motive-force— liberty. Decentralize teaching, create independent Universities, diversify the syllabuses, encourage a noble rivalry between the free minds of the masters, then you will be defending lay teaching by means of a fertilizing freedom. I admit that the reactionaries may be able to profit, for a time, from the general freedom, because their forces have been strongly organized for centuries, whereas agreement for individual emancipation is necessarily uncertain and difficult for unorganized, recently emancipated people to attain. But it is nevertheless certain that apprenticeship in liberty can only be served through liberty." The same article went on to quote with approval one Léopold Lacour who had said : " Side by side with instruction in the narrow sense there is education proper, which we have always too much neglected. In our State secondary schools, even in our private colleges, the pupils once they get out of the classroom find no other moral sanction than the fear of punishment ; there is no ideal to live by, no friendship between the pedagogue and the child. What is needed is a paternal solicitude leading to a sort of filial piety." Clemenceau's conclusion was as follows : " To struggle against the Church there is only one means—the liberty of the individual. A unified educational system is the negation of liberty. *Dispersez la parole* under independent Universities, set up living schools, so that there may be a free play of minds everywhere. Break up the scholastic barracks, and let the boarders scatter into little groups in the houses of the masters, where they can find a family, as in England, Switzerland, Germany."

It was not so much what Combes did as what he neglected to do that aroused Clemenceau's criticism. The Little Father was the most parochial of politicians. He had no more interest in international affairs than the seminarists with whom he had been brought up, and he left the whole business of foreign policy to Delcassé, who was Foreign Minister throughout the seven years between 1898 and 1905. Delcassé's policy was to build up the strongest possible connection with Russia, Italy, Spain and Britain. He expanded the Franco-Russian accord of 1891 and the military convention of 1893 into a virtual alliance, signed in 1899. He wooed Italy so successfully that her engagement to Germany and Austria-Hungary to support them in the event of French

127

aggression was to all practical intents and purposes broken. He won Spain over and was on
the verge of signing a Franco-Spanish entente
when he realized that a lasting agreement with
Spain depended on Britain's good will. With
Britain he had inherited a difficult situation.
When he came into office in 1898 there was an
ugly incident in the Sudan, where a French
expedition under Marchand clashed with the
British under Kitchener at Fashoda, a clash which
led the jingo Press of both countries to clamour
for war. Delcassé climbed down and set about
building up a Franco-British entente from the
bottom. The bottom in this case meant Morocco,
where the crumbling Empire of the Sultan offered
a tempting *Lebensraum* to European Powers.
Delcassé had had his eye on Morocco from the
beginning. His pact with Italy was based on it.
He had edged Italy out of Morocco by recognizing her claims on Libya. His pact with Spain
was based on a recognition of Spanish claims to
the zone of Tangier. In 1902 he went to England
with a proposal that France would give Britain
a free hand in Egypt and the Sudan in return for
Britain's recognition that France should have a
free hand in Morocco. The Entente with Britain
was signed in 1904, with a secret clause to this
effect. Germany was not consulted at any stage
in these negotiations, though as a signatory to
the international convention of 1880 she was a
joint guarantor of the sovereignty of the Sultan

and had a right to be consulted before any action was taken by a European Power in the Moroccan Empire.

It might be expected that Clemenceau would have supported Delcassé's policy. At the beginning he had given it his approval. " The brutal fact is," he wrote of the Fashoda incident, " that France cannot think of throwing herself into war for the possession of some African marshes while the German is encamped in Metz and Strasbourg." But soon he came into the open as an opponent of Delcassé. He distrusted the secret agreements with Tsarist Russia. He disliked the way in which Delcassé went about securing the understanding with England over Morocco. He had always opposed colonial ventures, and was not surprised when the German worm turned in 1905 and the Kaiser arrived at Tangier to claim Germany's treaty-rights in the Sultan's Empire. Delcassé had overreached himself. He could not go forward without the risk of war with Germany ; he could not go back without repudiating his whole policy. There was nothing for it but to resign. Clemenceau rejoiced at his fall. He allowed Delcassé no credit for having kept the friendship of both Britain and Russia during the difficult days of the Boer war and the Japanese war, or for having bought the support of Italy and Spain at a low price, or for leaving France as one of a group of four among the six Great Powers of Europe.

In foreign policy Clemenceau could not take his eyes away from Alsace-Lorraine, and this led him to fall foul of the idealists in the Bloc. The Radicals were more interested in purging the Army of Catholic officers than in building up a strong national defence. The Socialists were busy burying the hatchet with Germany. Jaurès and Francis de Pressensé were for abandoning all insistence on France's claim to the lost provinces. Clemenceau took them sharply to task. " To accept finally the rape of Alsace-Lorraine would be to diminish the essence of France's moral position," he told Jaurès. " I do not consent to the weakening of my country," he replied to Pressensé. " On the contrary, I mean to increase its military force. Not by means of the ' militarism ' of which I am accused (the militarism of our parade-ground armies was precisely the cause of Sedan), but by a better use of our man-power and money-power, which our beribboned military chiefs have squandered ever since the return from Sedan, by maintaining abuses which are everlasting sources of weakness."

The Bloc des Gauches, like its spiritual heir the Front Populaire thirty-two years later, broke down over foreign policy and national defence. Combes fell in 1904, his position undermined by a scandal in the War Ministry. Rather than take the word of Catholic generals on the suitability of candidates for staff appointments, the War Ministry had used the Grand Orient Lodge of

Free-Masons as a clearing-house for information on the characters and politico-religious convictions of officers. This was too much, even for an anti-clerical Chamber. Combes's successor, the financier Rouvier, took foreign policy into his own hands. Intent on liquidating the Tangier incident, he agreed to an international conference at Algeciras to settle the Moroccan question, and got rid of Delcassé, putting Pichon into the Ministry of Foreign Affairs. Pichon was Clemenceau's protégé, and the smile was on the face of the Tiger. But observers found it hard to understand Clemenceau's attitude during these years : it seemed so wildly contradictory—a Dreyfusard wanting a strong Army and preaching the doctrine of the *Revanche*, while at the same time opposing Delcassé's moves towards a crypto-coalition against Germany. What had happened to Clemenceau ?

There were three possible explanations. The first was that he was old and failing. Had he not said in the Senate speech of December 1903 : " I will explain to you in all simplicity and in all frankness the state of mind of a man who has been in National Assemblies for a very long time and who is now approaching the end of his career " ? (Certainly, he was never to feel as old as he felt now, in his sixty-third year.) The second was that he hated Socialism more than he loved progress. There was evidence for this, too : " I make a distinction between the Socialist

131

critique and the constructive policy of Socialism. The Socialist critique is necessary to the Republic ... but the Socialist party is also an *étatiste* party. It does not talk about State monopoly, it talks about Collectivism ; but they are the same creed." The third explanation was that Clemenceau was growing up : the iconoclast was becoming constructive, the polemicist was realizing the complexity of things, the politician was turning into a statesman. Which explanation was nearest to the truth, the future would reveal.

Chapter Seven

The Making of a Government

WHEN Clemenceau accepted the office of Minister of Home Affairs in March 1906, everybody was surprised. He had hitherto refused every government post that had been offered, and there was nothing in the programme of M. Sarrien's ministry that seemed likely to attract him. The only apparent reason for his accepting responsibility for Home Affairs under Sarrien was that the circumstances of the moment were particularly critical.

An explosion of fire-damp in the Courrières-Lens mines had cost the lives of 1,150 workers underground ; it was the greatest disaster that had ever occurred in the mining industry. The miners came out on strike, furious with the owners whose failure to enforce the most elementary safety precautions seemed to be the obvious cause of the tragedy. Everything pointed to a riot, and the mayor and deputy of the district were asking the Government to send down a hundred thousand troops immediately. " I will go myself," said Clemenceau, " I will tell the miners that their rights will be respected as fully as those of the owners, provided that there is no disorder.

Democracy is the art of disciplining oneself."
And he went to Lens, unaccompanied, to interview the Strike Committees and to harangue
the miners.

It was magnificent, but it was not politics.
Clemenceau failed to convince the miners, as he
had failed to convince every crowd of working
men, from the morning on the Butte of Montmartre to the evening at Salernes. His case was
perfectly logical. The miners had the right to
strike ; he would guarantee it. The blacklegs
had the right to work ; he would protect them,
with State troops if necessary. The owners had
the right to their property ; he would put troops
in the pits to see that there was no sabotage. All
this was fully consonant with the Rights of Man
and with Republican principles, but it would not
do for the miners. They saw in Clemenceau,
not the agitator who had gone down to Carmaux
to take up the strikers' cause with Millerand and
Pelletan in 1892, or the sympathetic inquirer
who had gone to Anzin with a Parliamentary
commission in 1884, but the agent of *les plus forts*,
the minister calling in the Army to blunt the edge
of the workers' only weapon and serve the interests
of mineowners whose carelessness had been
responsible for the disaster and of shareholders
who had been making 1,000 per cent. profit.
The strike spread and soon there was bloodshed :
troops escorting a group of blacklegs were
stoned by the mob, with the result that several

soldiers were wounded and one young officer killed.

Strikes are contagious. Before the Lens uproar was over, the electrical engineers of Paris went on strike. Suddenly at six o'clock one evening the current was switched off. The Underground was brought to a standstill and threatened with flooding, and two million Parisians were left rummaging for candles. Clemenceau acted without hesitation. He ordered military engineers to take charge, under Army control. The lights went on again, and the strike was broken.

A famous *interpellation* followed in the Chamber, one of the most dramatic debates in French parliamentary history. The issue was the rights of organized workers against those of private monopoly, and the relation of the State to the conflicting interests. The protagonists were the two greatest statesmen that the Third Republic ever produced—Jaurès the architect of Socialism, the unchallenged leader of the French Socialist party and, for that matter, of the international workers' movement; Clemenceau the archetype of individualism, the lifelong Radical who had championed the weak against the strong in every crisis since 1870.

With a sense of delighted anticipation the deputies settled down to hear the orators make their bid for the Radicals' vote. In appearance and manner the two men presented a striking

135

contrast—Jaurès sanguine and benign, with close-cropped hair and grizzled beard, a Frenchman of the Midi, a Latin, unrolling his balanced periods with faultless rhythm and communicating an enthusiasm, a sense of inspiration, which against another opponent would have been irresistible ; Clemenceau sallow, bitter and bald, a hard-headed Celt, using words only to cauterize or to cut. Jaurès' case was that the Government had no programme. They were playing for safety, sitting on the fence. Now that Combes had drawn the teeth of clericalism the Radicals had become indistinguishable from Conservatives, no more anxious than they to complete the work of the Revolution by adding economic to political democracy. He concluded with a formidable *argumentum ad hominem*, accusing Clemenceau of " interfering with the very right to strike which you yourself have declared to be sacred. You are using the military discipline of the comrades of the men out on strike against the electrical companies in order to render their protest nugatory by employing the sappers against them. You have, in fact, called out the powers of the State to crush the workers in a particular industry. If you were true to yourself, you would convert the electrical supply of Paris, now in the hands of grasping monopolists, into a public service and give the strikers every satisfaction. That is the only real solution to social anarchy."

It was true that Clemenceau had gone back

on his professions. In the early days he had demanded " the liquidation of the great railway, canal and mining companies, and the exploitation of those industries by and for the profit of those who work in them. In *La Mêlée sociale* he had written in favour of Socialism : " Socialism is social altruism in action ; it is the intervention of all against the murderous activities (*vitalité meurtrière*) of the few. To hold, as the economists do, that one ought to oppose the effort of social altruism, is to misunderstand mankind ; it is a calumny. To complain that collective action will lessen the liberty of the individual, is to protest in favour of the liberty of the strongest, which spells oppression. . . . We take our stand on the solid basis of the rights of the individual, and we invoke State interference only in order to guarantee, defend and protect the individual against the violences of coalitions of interests." But now the case was altered. Clemenceau was no longer a critic, he was a minister ; after a quarter of a century in opposition, he was at last in power, and power is sweet.

Rising to reply to Jaurès' interpellation, Clemenceau based his case on law and his arguments on a *tu quoque.* At Lens he had protected the right of the miners to strike and of the blacklegs to work. He had called in the troops, but he had ordered them not to fire ; the only casualty was an officer, a young servant of the Republic, murdered by the mob. " Were

137

M. Jaurès to become Minister of the Interior—misfortune comes so suddenly—he would himself send down troops to stop wholesale pillage. Yet, if he did, he would be denounced in his turn by the anarchical leaders of the General Confederation of Labour as the enemy of the class whose cause he now champions. I challenge M. Jaurès to say what he would do in circumstances such as those which I have had to face ! " There was no answer. Clemenceau went on to answer Jaurès' accusation that the Radicals lacked a positive policy. " When M. Jaurès from the height of the tribune asked what was my programme I had difficulty in refraining from jumping up to say : ' My programme ? It is in your pocket ; you have taken it from me ! ! ' . . . I am a supporter in principle of the eight-hour day, but I want to reach it by stages and not by the brusque substitution of a uniform and compulsory eight hours in place of eleven. I am a supporter of the income tax. . . . I am a supporter of the return of the great monopolies to the State. Ah, but one moment : I do not say that I will have them taken over by the State to-morrow. We will content ourselves with making reforms in good time and at the right moment. For a start, we will begin by buying back certain of the railway companies."

Clemenceau in office had turned into an Opportunist. He concluded his speech by an open challenge to the Socialists. " Either re-

forms or revolution ! We have made reforms.
We want to go on making them. If you intend
to work with us, we offer you our hand. If you
refuse, let each of us go our own way." From
now on there could be nothing in common
between Clemenceau and the Socialists. It was
a tragedy for France that he and Jaurès should
have become opponents. They had worked so
fruitfully together over the Dreyfus affair and in
the Combes days. The Socialist leader was so
nearly a Radical, the Radical leader so nearly
a Socialist. But Clemenceau's temperament
barred him from the Socialist fold : he could
never accept Party discipline ; he could never
suffer fools or even wise men gladly ; his sceptical
gorge rose at the Utopianism of the Socialists—
" Do you know how to spot an article by Jaurès ?
All the verbs are in the future tense." His
temperament debarred him, too, from any personal sympathy with Jaurès—"Jaurès, so eloquent,
and Clemenceau did not like eloquence; he liked
the short, sharp word. Jaurès, so kind, and
Clemenceau did not like kindness ; if he loved
anything in the world (which is doubtful) it was
Justice, the old Roman justice, generator of war.
Jaurès, so hopeful, and Clemenceau did not like
hopefulness ; he liked action, combat, victory, if
victory were possible and, if not, defeat ; a good
defeat never frightened him." (The quotation
is from Daniel Halévy.) And the breach had
more than temperament behind it. Clemenceau

and the Radicals in general had no contact with the industrial or even with the agricultural masses. They had no contact or sympathy with working-class movements outside France. Their political philosophy had got little further than the ideas of 1789. " The Socialist principle," said Clemenceau now, " is the abandonment of individualism. Socialist principles are the abandonment of the Rights of Man proclaimed by the French Revolution."

The breach was not yet final. The Socialist party would continue to support the Radicals in power so long as there were signs of reforms being put into practice. The Radicals, however, were by far the strongest parliamentary group, particularly after the elections of 1906. Clemenceau could do what he liked so long as he had his own party solidly behind him.

In October Clemenceau became Prime Minister. He had waited a long time, but he was only sixty-five—younger than Disraeli had been on first attaining full power. The public waited with interest for him to announce the names of his colleagues : this cabinet-breaker turned cabinet-maker, how would he act ? He acted like a man who means to be master in his own house, choosing tools rather than colleagues. Picquart at the War Ministry, Thomson at the Admiralty, Ruan at the Ministry of Justice and Pichon at the Foreign Office would do as they were told. Briand, retained as Minister of

Education, Briand's friend Barthou put in as
Minister of Public Works, Viviani in the newly-
created Ministry of Labour would keep some of
their old followers on the Left quiet and would
give no trouble, especially as Clemenceau retained
the Home Office himself. To the general second-
rateness of this cabinet of Radical yes-men and
pseudo-Socialists there was only one exception
besides Clemenceau. Caillaux at the Ministry
of Finance might go his own way, but the new
Premier knew nothing about finance, and it was
just as well to have someone who did at the
Exchequer, even if he were as vain and unapproachable as Joseph Caillaux.

Clemenceau's first Ministry ran straight into
trouble. The strike epidemic spread to the
Nantes dockers, to the Fougères boot-makers, to
the Grenoble metal-workers and then to the
peasants of the Midi. The last was by far the
most formidable. The import of cheap Algerian
wine threatened to ruin the French wine-growers ;
they could get no more than ten francs the hecto-
litre—a derisory price. In June they came out
on strike, demonstrated in hundreds of thousands
at Béziers, at Montpellier, and at Narbonne
where they set fire to Government buildings.
The 17th Infantry Regiment was ordered to fire
on the rioters at Narbonne, but the soldiers were
local lads whose fathers were among the rioters ;
they refused to obey. Mutiny was followed
by civil defiance : three hundred mayors of

communes in Languedoc called a general strike, refusing to pay taxes. Clemenceau acted as his old enemy Thiers would have done : he sent in fresh troops. Then, by a personal touch of which Thiers would have been incapable, he sent for the peasants' leader, Marcellin Albert, a Gandhi-esque figure known in the South as The Redeemer, and talked him round, concluding the interview by lending him a couple of hundred francs for his fare home.

The troubles in the Midi ended, but the strike epidemic was not over. The sandpit workers of Vigneux came out and the Parisian public were offered the spectacle of troops being sent to quell them. The Paris postmen came out, and after a moment of hesitation Clemenceau was heard laying down the law that civil servants had no right to strike. For civil servants to strike was a crime against the State and that, it appeared, was deadly sin. At any rate, Clemenceau arrested the leaders. The poacher had turned gamekeeper with a vengeance.

But Clemenceau's main preoccupation was not with domestic but with foreign affairs. He had inherited an awkward legacy from Delcassé. The great nations of Europe were lined up in opposing diplomatic camps, with the Central Powers in the stronger position. Whatever doubts there might be about their Italian ally, Germany and Austria-Hungary were both better armed and more ready to use their arms than the members

142

of the Triple Entente. " I have always thought,"
Clemenceau wrote in *L'Aurore* a year before taking
office, " that an implacable fatality from which
we cannot escape will some day force out the
military weapon which the Germans forged when
they founded their Empire upon the battlefield."
War is inevitable, he insisted in a letter to
Georges Louis in September 1908, " I have
written as much—which was perhaps unneces-
sary. We must do nothing to provoke it, but we
must be ready to wage it."

There were two international danger-spots, the
Balkans, where the interests of Austria and Russia
clashed, and Morocco, where those of Germany
and France were in conflict. Both were perilously
inflamed during the time of Clemenceau's
Ministry. In 1908 Austria suddenly annexed
the Slav provinces of Bosnia and Herzegovina,
thereby presenting Russia with a *fait accompli*
which she had no alternative but to accept. In
the same year trouble flared out again in Morocco.
The Algeciras Conference, while recognizing the
" independence " of the Sultan, had set up a
State Bank under the joint influence of Britain,
Spain, France and Germany, and a police force
for Morocco under Spain and France. The
French used their police privileges for imperialist
ends. In 1908 Sultan Abd-el-Aziz, who was the
puppet of France and therefore vastly unpopular
with his subjects, was deposed by his brother
Moulay Hafid whom Clemenceau firmly believed

to be in the pay of Germany. Relations between France and Germany were therefore sorely strained and the inevitable "incident" followed a few months later, when three German deserters from the Foreign Legion were arrested while trying to board a German ship in Casablanca, and two German Consular officials accompanying them were illtreated by French soldiers. The German authorities claimed the right to protect their nationals and the German and French Press took up the affair *fortissimo*. Clemenceau's view was that the case should go before the Court of International Justice at The Hague. The German Government made no objection to this, but sent its ambassador in Paris, von Radolin, to ask the French Government for an apology for the treatment of the Consular officials. Clemenceau received the ambassador politely but refused point-blank. The story goes that von Radolin then said that he would find himself in the regrettable position of having to ask for his passports ; to which Clemenceau, looking at his watch, replied : "Your Excellency, the train for Cologne leaves at nine o'clock. It is now seven. You have just time."

The story was vouched for by Clemenceau himself in later years, but its veracity may be doubted, for his whole policy at this time was to avoid anything that might provoke war. He refused an apology for the Casablanca incident, but he chose arbitration rather than a downright insistence on French rights. He took a firm line against Moulay and encouraged Lyautey to pursue a forward policy in Morocco, but he allowed an agreement for Moroccan development to be made behind the scenes between the German armament firm of Krupp and the French firm of Schneider.

Knowing that France was in no condition to fight alone, he devoted himself to building up the strength of her alliances. It was difficult for him, the lifelong critic of the Republic's alliance with the Tsar, to do much to build up Franco-Russian friendship, but that little he did. From the moment he came into office he dropped all criticism of the Tsar's government and tried to promote friendly relations, both financial and diplomatic. A loan of 2,250 million francs, floated in Paris in 1906, greased the wheels of diplomacy so effectively that a new clause was written in to the Franco-Russian alliance providing for immediate mobilization by both Powers in the event of German mobilization. Clemenceau had Russia where he wanted her ; his problem now was to bring Britain into line.

He had seen from the beginning what form the Anglo-French *rapprochement* should take. Understanding the English dislike of " entangling alliances "—as acute before 1914 as the American dislike was to be afterwards—he had gone to London in 1891 to put before Joseph Chamberlain an unofficial proposal for what he called an

145

entente cordiale of the two peoples. Chamberlain
and Salisbury had turned a cold shoulder. But
fifteen years later, with the Liberals in power,
the British War Office worked out a project for
sending 100,000 troops to France and Belgium
within a fortnight of any German invasion.
Clemenceau's task as Prime Minister was to turn
this secret military plan into a definite political
undertaking. He took every opportunity—jour-
neys to London to see Campbell-Bannerman,
Asquith and Haldane, visits to King Edward at
Marienbad, interviews with prominent English
journalists—to ram home the point that unless
Britain were strongly armed and prepared for a
campaign on the Continent, France would be
overrun by Germany, and Britain left with no
bulwarks but her navy. " I visited him in 1907,"
wrote J. A. Spender, " to receive a long, and to me
surprising, lecture on the danger to France of
the understanding with Great Britain. A war
with Germany, he said, was a far more serious
possibility for France than for us. We should
win an easy victory at sea, while she would be
invaded and her territory devastated. We must
therefore not presume that France would follow
us blindly into war with Germany on the naval
issue. It was for years his theme that Britain
would only be a safe ally for France if she armed
herself with a conscript army on the continental
pattern and accepted all the liabilities of war on
land as well as on sea. Otherwise all the return

blows of Anglo-German quarrel would fall on France. Again and again he reverted to this theme, and all through these years he seemed to regard the *Entente* as a strictly experimental and rather dangerous *mariage de convenance*, which was to be judged solely from the point of view of French interests and French security."

In August 1908, when he was on his annual holiday at Carlsbad, Clemenceau made the same point with considerably greater force to Wickham Steed of *The Times*. "We know that on the morrow of the outbreak of war between Germany and England, the German armies will invade France by way of Belgium, and that Germany will seek in France an indemnity for the losses likely to be suffered on sea at the hands of England. What can England do to help us? Destroy the German Fleet? That would make a pretty hole in the water! In 1870 there was no German Fleet, but the Prussians entered Paris all the same. . . . I am convinced that our position will be one of extreme danger until England has a national army worth the name. A hundred thousand men in Belgium would not be much good, but 250,000 or 500,000 would change the course of the war. As it is, England could not send 100,000 without the greatest difficulty." Clemenceau repeated this to Edward VII at Marienbad a few days later. The King was impressed. "Clemenceau," he remarked, "is a true friend of his own country and of ours."

Domestic affairs left Clemenceau little time for the conduct of foreign policy. The lay-laws of Combes's Ministry had left formidable problems of administration. After the disestablishment of the Church, acute disputes arose over the apportionment and control of Church property. Inventories were being drawn up and Catholics were up in arms against the sacrilege of valuing holy vessels and ornaments. Clemenceau played for safety and cancelled the inventories—" totting up vases and candlesticks isn't worth one human life." But the religious controversy went on, and when the Pope refused to allow the French clergy to apply to the civil authorities for permission to hold Church services, there was nothing to be done but to cancel the laws demanding civil authorization of all forms of public meeting. Clemenceau felt that the substance of victory over clericalism had indeed been won ; he could afford to make concessions over trifles.

But if the clerical question could be left to solve itself, the social question most certainly could not. The General Confederation of Labour (usually known as the C.G.T., the French equivalent of the T.U.C.) had adopted a new Charter in 1905 announcing contempt for such piecemeal reforms as parliamentary action could bring and pinning its faith to revolutionary action by means of the general strike. Unlike their British *confrères*, the French trade unionists were more extreme than the parliamentary

148

Socialist Party, and the constitution of the C.G.T., unlike that of the T.U.C., gave disproportionate authority to the extremist elements. They despised their ex-champion Briand, and were not always susceptible to the charms of Jaurès, who was often sorely embarrassed at having to defend in parliament acts of violence which were the inevitable consequence of the policy of ill-timed strikes. They extended their influence among the schoolteachers and other minor civil servants. Worst of all from Clemenceau's point of view, the French trade-union movement was opposed to conscription ; it saw the Army as the instrument of capitalism and issued a *Manuel du soldat* attacking military discipline.

All this was bound to bring out the tiger in Clemenceau. His attitude towards strikes became increasingly repressive, and when the C.G.T. took up the cause of the Vigneux labourers and rather tentatively proclaimed a general strike, he retaliated by arresting Métivier and other trade-union leaders. By this time the extreme Left, both in parliament and outside, was so angry that some measure of social reform could no longer be postponed. Clemenceau therefore proposed and negotiated the nationalization of the Western Railway. The Socialists were delighted, and so were the shareholders who were bought out at a fantastic price. The project was under discussion for some years before the Railway was finally acquired by the State in 1910

CLEMENCEAU

and during that period the directors had let the permanent way, rolling stock and buildings fall into such disrepair that the line would have to be run at a loss to the taxpayers for many years.

This first major reform of the Clemenceau Ministry was also to be its last. Caillaux had a plan for a progressive tax on incomes, which would end the inequitable system by which direct taxes were levied on the rent of the taxpayer's residence and business premises instead of on his revenue. The income tax had always been a plank in the Republican platform, but Clemenceau did not like it. Or perhaps he did not like Caillaux. In any case he gave his Finance Minister no support and the Bill was thrown out by the Senate (which never included a single Socialist member until after 1918) after being passed by the Chamber. Five years were to pass before the income-tax Bill got through the Senate and four more before it came into operation, and even then with so many loopholes and exemptions (persons engaged in agriculture, for instance, were exempt) that it could hardly be called an income tax at all.

A reform which might be expected to have lain nearer to Clemenceau's heart—the reorganization and rearmament of the Services—similarly came to nothing. There was some tightening of the conscription regulations, some reform of the artillery, a reconstruction of the Ecole de Guerre

150

at the head of which Clemenceau put a Colonel Foch, but the budget allocations for the Armed Forces were cut to the bone. In 1907 the Service Estimates were for 73 million francs ; they were reduced to 60 millions. In 1908 the Estimates were for 88 millions ; the sum granted was 57 millions. In 1909 the Services asked for 98 millions ; they got 66 millions. Germany was spending three times as much. It is understandable that a Parliament in which Socialist and Radicals were so numerous should have been against military expenditure, but it is difficult to see why Clemenceau acquiesced in the cutting of his minister's estimates.

At the same time the French Navy was falling into disrepute. A series of disasters in the dockyards led to a Commission of Inquiry, presided over by Delcassé, which forced the resignation of Thomson from the Ministry. A second commission, with more extensive terms of reference, produced a report accusing the Government of negligence. When Delcassé, presenting the report in the Chamber, asked the Government to justify its stewardship, Clemenceau chose to turn the matter into a personal issue. Although Delcassé's anti-German policy had differed in no essential respect from his own, he hated the little man. He lashed Delcassé with his tongue, chiding him for the climb-down at Algeciras, taunting him with having humiliated France. The deputies, astonished and shocked, supported

151

Delcassé by 212 votes to 196. Whereupon Clemenceau immediately resigned.

The fall of Clemenceau from office was as surprising as his accession had been. Forgetting that democracy is the art of disciplining oneself, he had flung out in a huff at a moment when his Ministry was in no real peril and when foreign affairs, if not the domestic situation, seemed to demand his leadership. France set herself to conduct a sort of inquest on the Tiger. Was he a great man, or was he not? He had certainly kept his Ministry in being for a long time—for two years and nine months, in fact (no Government of the Third Republic had ever lasted for three years ; the average duration during the period 1875-1914 was under ten months). He had apparently stood up to Germany over the Casablanca affair and had strengthened the Entente with England. He had created the Ministry of Labour and had nationalized the Western Railway and provided pensions for some railway-workers. But he had shown a most extraordinary frivolity of attitude, seeming to glory in his intransigent resignation : " I came in with an umbrella," he remarked, " I go out with a stick," and he strode out of the Chamber to dine with Debussy and Fauré. He had treated his colleagues outrageously, bullying Pichon, despising Briand and Barthou, neglecting Picquart and Thomson, overruling them all. By his onslaught on Delcassé he seemed to bear out the saying of

Jaurès that " he would trample on France herself in order to get at close quarters with an adversary." He had shown an utter incapacity to attend to detail. He might have studied the income-tax project with Caillaux and have championed the Bill in parliament, lending it such authority that the Senate would at least have nominated a favourable commission, but he neither supported nor repudiated his Finance Minister.

As an old parliamentary hand it would not have been difficult for him to guide Chamber and Senate round this and other corners, but he seemed to prefer to goad them. He forgot that Parliament, like the traditional schoolchild, can be led but not driven. Maurice Barrès, meditating on this in his journal, wrote : " For the proper management of a Parliament or a Government, as for the proper management of a horse, a calming influence is needed : the best and truest mastery is to placate, not to offend. M. Clemenceau is the type of driver of which we have too many among our Paris cabbies, a driver embittered by the intemperance of the seasons (and what bitter, terrible winters he has seen !) and made half-mad with pride in the high solitude of his box-seat. Blows of the whip, cruel wrenches of the rein, a prodigious litany of oaths and abuse. The parliamentary horse foams with impotence ; the tax-paying fares, who at first laughed at the liveliness of his driving, get alarmed. The Society for the

153

Prevention of Cruelty to Animals, watching from the pavement, lifts despairing arms to heaven. Good citizens begin to look round for a policeman."

Worst of all, Clemenceau seemed to have lost all sense of direction. The lifelong apostle of *la Revanche*, he had starved the armed forces of money ; the traditional enemy of colonial adventures, he occupied Morocco ; the sworn adversary of State monopoly, he nationalized (at a price) the Western Railway ; the champion of workers' rights, he sent in troops to break strike after strike. Clemenceau had always held that the direction of the Republic must lie through administrative decentralization and through union of the progressive parties in parliament. " Not only do I stand firm for decentralization, but my ideal of government is Federalism," he had written in *l'Aurore* in 1903, " so far am I from meriting the reproach of Jacobin sin which the *Temps* hurls at random at all who are not of its sect. The ancient division into provinces, which was the product of history, was destroyed by the Revolution in a moment of anger in order to break resistance to the new order by the combined forces of the old. It came about that in hastening the realization of their system of authoritarian liberation, the Jacobins, to use the term employed by the *Temps*, chiefly succeeded in forging the instruments of Napoleonic despotism. . . . We have proclaimed the Republic, but we have not made it." So far from making the Republic while he was in office, so far from reforming even the centralized Napoleonic civil service, Clemenceau made use of the worst features of Napoleonic administration. The police spy and the *agent provocateur* flourished during his four years as Minister of the Interior. Métivier, the trade-union secretary whom he arrested and denounced as the chief instigator of the strikes, was an agent employed at a regular salary by the police. During the term of imprisonment which Clemenceau insisted that he should serve so as to prevent suspicion from arising among trade-unionists, he was paid a double salary. The friend of Blanqui had become the imitator of Fouché.

It was the same with the principle of Left-solidarity in parliament. Clemenceau had now been going out of his way to make enemies on the Left as he had always done to make enemies on the Right. The Bloc des Gauches which arose out of the Dreyfus affair gave the Republic the three strongest and longest-lived of its Ministries—those of Waldeck-Rousseau, Combes and Clemenceau himself. But Clemenceau broke the Bloc by antagonizing the Socialists and by splitting his own Radical party. The more extreme Radicals broke away into splinter groups on the Left and voted with the Socialists against him. Clemenceau got into the habit of relying on shifting majorities made up of varying party

155.

combinations, including Right-wing as well as Centre elements. The new system secured its purpose for a time, particularly when manipulated by such skilful hands as those of Briand who succeeded Clemenceau in power ; but it postponed indefinitely the social and economic reforms which the Bloc had been formed to promote. Not until the Front Populaire came into office in 1936 would France have an opportunity to take up the task of the old Left coalition.

In place of a policy he had adopted a sort of Satanic pose. " After all," he had said to Jaurès as the House was emptying after the 1906 debate, " you are not God Almighty," and Jaurès answered : " And you, Clemenceau, are not even the Devil." Yet one cannot help feeling that Clemenceau represented Original Sin and Jaurès the Divine Afflatus in French politics. There was something Mephistophelian about him in those years, a *Schadenfreude*, a devilish pleasure in hurting his potential friends.

Barrès, most acute of contemporary observers, noted : " He no longer believes in anything but himself." It was not true. Clemenceau always loved and believed in three things : having his own way, Republican ideas and France. The insolent, aristocratic tendencies of his adolescence had hardened into a passion for power, but he realized that he could get no justification for that passion apart from an affectionate response, and that response was lacking in the France of

1909. His Republican ideas proved inapplicable to present discontents ; in the strike-crises he had no principle to fall back on except an undeveloped interpretation of the Rights of Man. The situation in France between 1906 and 1910 provided no scope for Clemenceau's lay religion. He had foreseen the impasse when he wrote in *Au Fil des jours* : " Will people blame the Radical and Socialist deputies for their failure in strike-crises ? What will people say if they refuse to answer the call of the workers ? The imperfection of the bosses will not be the only factor; there will also be the imperfection of the masses." The new social movements were in the direction of commercial concentration or of Socialist revolution, and each was equally detestable to him, for the same reasons as to Mill. (In 1848 Mill had written : " Various schemes for managing the productive resources of the country by public instead of private agency . . . are at present workable only by an *élite* of mankind, and have yet to prove their power of training mankind at large to the state of improvement which they presuppose." And in 1861 : " We saw clearly that to render any such social transformation either possible or desirable, an equivalent change of character must take place both in the uncultivated herd who now compose the labouring masses, and in the immense majority of the employers. Both these classes must learn by practice to labour and combine for generous, or at any rate for public and social purposes, and not, as hitherto, solely for narrowly interested ones.") Barrès was right in saying that " he is in fact superstitious about the present form of society ; he pretends to despise it, he maligns it, he attacks it, but that is all pretence." The march of time had turned Radicalism into Conservatism ; Clemenceau's ideas were out of date.

There remained only France and his growing desire to serve her simply, singly, with all his heart. One day, perhaps, the day would come. Jaurès had an intimation of it when he told the Chamber in February 1909, while Clemenceau was still in office : " There is an English journal— *The Fortnightly Review*—which the Prime Minister knows well and on which he has many friends or at any rate admirers. The other day this review, examining in an important article the respective chances of France and Germany in the event of a conflict, said : ' Germany has sixty million inhabitants, France only fifty million—but she has M. Clemenceau.' And the article went on : ' In a possible conflict he will be one of the greatest War Ministers that history has ever known.' " The deputies laughed.

Clemenceau shrugged himself out of office : " Having destroyed every Ministry for thirty years, I ended by destroying my own." He went to Carlsbad for the cure. He went to Bernouville where he had taken a country house so as to be near Monet at Giverny. In the summer of 1910 he accepted an invitation to tour Brazil and Argentina, lecturing on Democracy. (The organizers had originally invited Kubelik, the violinist ; when Kubelik refused they asked Jaurès ; Clemenceau was the third choice.) The tour was not a great success ; Clemenceau was a poor lecturer. He published a little travel-book, *Notes de Voyages dans l'Amérique du Sud*, a pot-boiler and the worst he ever wrote. These two years did not add to his reputation as an elder statesman.

Before the end of 1911 he was back in the political fray. The Moroccan question had flared up again. The French Government had sent troops to occupy Fez in May, in contradiction of their declared intentions of acting in concert with the other Algeciras signatories. The Germans replied by sending a cruiser to Agadir to stake out their claim. It was the Tangier crisis all over again, but this time France had a cunning man at the helm. Caillaux saw his way to do a deal with Germany and secretly negotiated a treaty giving Germany a right of way to the Congo River in return for a free hand for France in Morocco. This was too much for Clemenceau. A policy of non-provocation was one thing, but appeasement was another. He disapproved of the Fez expedition as of anything else that would take the French army away from French soil, and he had no use for the Moroccan Protectorate which was the inevitable if unavowed object of

Caillaux' policy, but he was a thousand times more antagonistic to dividing colonial spoils at the dictate of Germany. In the Senate Commission on Morocco, of which Raymond Poincaré was chairman, he attacked Caillaux for having negotiated a treaty over the head of the Foreign Minister, de Selves. " True, we want peace in order to build up our country, but if war is thrust upon us we shall be found ready. Germany thinks that world domination lies for her in the folds of victory ; defeat for us would mean that we would be her perpetual vassals. We are pacificists, or rather pacific, but we are not yet the under-dogs." Caillaux tried to save his Ministry by allowing de Selves to resign ; his idea was to appoint Delcassé in his stead, but Clemenceau would not hear of it and Caillaux himself had to resign.

It was quite like the old days of the 'eighties. But Clemenceau was over seventy now, and a very sick man. He underwent an operation, dangerous in those days, on the prostate gland. Surprisingly, he made a perfect recovery. Henceforth all his time was given to a new paper, *L'Homme libre*, which he founded with Georges Mandel, François Carco and Jean Martet as assistants, and to the gladiatorial games in parliament.

What Clemenceau wanted in those years is difficult to see. " The thing that struck me in 1870-1871," he told the Senate, " was the dissolution of old political and social links ; the leader had disappeared ; there was no longer any France, only a litter of Frenchmen. We had an invasion and profound political divisions. The Catholic Church alone remained standing. How did the country recover ? The Republican Party made contact with the new public spirit. It remade France." But where was the Republican Party now ? The Radicals had split—one faction, under Caillaux, working for an understanding with Germany, in which they were supported by Jaurès; another, under Briand and Barthou, seeking safety in numbers of conscripts and proposing to increase the term of compulsory service from two years to three. The strongest man in France was Poincaré, who had succeeded Caillaux as Premier, a dour reserved company-lawyer of unimpeachable integrity and no party affiliations. With the war-clouds gathering over Europe, France needed a strong man at the helm, and Poincaré was the obvious successor to Fallières as President of the Republic. But Clemenceau hated Poincaré as he had hated Ferry, another Lorraine lawyer. He supported the candidature of Pams, a Radical nonentity whom he himself despised—" Pams is not a name, it's a noise." Poincaré was elected. It was a personal defeat for Clemenceau, who had never before failed to get his candidate elected to the Presidency. The Tiger seemed to be going on with his old game of opposition for opposition's sake. He overthrew Briand on the issue of electoral reform, he cheered when Premier followed Premier—Barthou, Doumergue, Ribot, Viviani—in impotent and rapid succession.

And then, when Clemenceau was seventy-three, the war came and with it another opportunity, of the kind which the 1870 invasion and the Dreyfus affair had given him, for finding himself and for saving France.

Chapter Eight

The Fourth Crisis : 1914-18

FRANCE all but lost the war in the first few weeks. Seven German armies, swinging like a gate on the hinge of the Metz fortress, brushed aside all opposition in Luxembourg and Belgium, swept on to Mons, on over the Somme, over the Aisne, over the Marne until their advanced patrols were within twelve miles of Paris.

There had been nothing resembling this momentum in the history of modern warfare, though to the French it seemed not unlike a nightmarish repetition of 1870. True, France this time was united : all parties had rallied to the support of Viviani's Government in a *Union Sacrée*. True, France was no longer alone : the British Expeditionary Force was in the field and had fought well at Mons ; the Russians had mobilized with unusual speed and had invaded East Prussia. But could France get through the August days ? Could the Germans be held on the Marne ?

Clemenceau was beside himself during these weeks. On the day war was declared he struck his keynote in *L'Homme libre* : " And now, to arms ! Everyone's chance will come : not a

child on our soil but will have his part in the
gigantic battle.[1] To die is nothing ; we must
conquer.   And for that we shall need every arm.
The weakest will have his part in the common
glory." He rushed to the presidential palace
and offered Poincaré his hand—" *mon cher ami*,"
he called him. He worked with the Government
to get Italy in on the Allies' side and worked on
them to urge the Russians into an offensive against
Austria and the Japanese into sending an army.
But the news of the defeats shook Clemenceau
out of his mood of reconciliation. Soon he was
lashing out in *L'Homme libre* against every form of
governmental action and inaction ; demanding
the heads of the " Jesuitical Generals " (Castel-
nau's in particular), whom Viviani would not
remove, insisting on the imprisonment of suspects
whom Malvy, the young Radical Minister of the
Interior, would not arrest ; seeing everywhere
complacency, indolence and incompetence
amounting to treachery, preaching everywhere
total war. Poincaré was in two minds about
whether to call on him to form a Ministry.
" There is no doubt whatever that in public
Clemenceau has gained ground in many points,"
he wrote in his diary on August 25th. " He
pleases a good many people by his unbounded
energy, his perfect coolness in the presence of

[1] His own son's chance came on August 14th when Michel
Clemenceau was wounded by a German officer's revolver
bullet ; he killed the officer.

danger, and even by the very roughness of his manner. But one never knows whether, if he were head of the Government, he would not try to substitute for military authority his own overwhelming and often capricious influence." Two days later the President was still undecided : " I am always rather nervous, perhaps a little too nervous, of his whims, his very versatility, and his fine contempt for everybody except himself. . . . It is certainly not for mere ambition that Clemenceau wants to be in office ; it is because he is convinced that he will save the country and that he alone can do so. If ever the real moment comes, I shall call on him without hesitation. The more I think of the matter, the more I say to myself : ' So long as victory is possible he is capable of upsetting everything ! A day will perhaps come when I shall add : ' Now that everything seems to be lost, he alone is capable of saving everything.' "

Suddenly and surprisingly, on the anniversary of Valmy, the tide turned. Joffre counterattacked, held the Germans on the Marne, forced them slowly back to the line of the Aisne. France was saved from immediate defeat.

In the relaxed mood following the victory of the Marne, the French Ministers turned on Clemenceau who had harried them so relentlessly. The one suggestion of his which they had accepted was the imposition of a strict censorship on military information. In practice, this soon turned into a censorship on opinion and on constructive criticism. Clemenceau's exposures of the disgraceful state of the French medical and hospital services came in for particularly ruthless blue pencilling. On September 29th the *Homme libre* was suspended altogether. Clemenceau replied by publishing a new paper on the following day ; its title was *L'Homme enchaîné*. The Government should have realized that he was irrepressible. After all, he was an elder statesman, the last survivor of the group of delegates who had voted at Bordeaux in 1871 against peace preliminaries with the Germans, the prophet who had consistently foretold renewed aggression by Germany. Viviani offered him a seat in the Cabinet, and Briand, Viviani's successor, renewed the offer, but Clemenceau saw this as an attempt to muzzle him, and refused. He had no use for office without power ; he could do better work for France outside the Government. He had a following in the country that was out of all proportion to his support in parliament.

L'Homme enchaîné became the most popular of all serious journals with the soldiers ; soon it was selling a hundred thousand copies a day. The Tiger's tone had something in it that went straight to the heart of the *poilu*. His growl, his brusquerie, his savage jousting was on the soldiers' level ; he echoed their contempt for brass-hats, red tape, bombastic oratory and

166

THE FOURTH CRISIS: 1914-18

incompetence in high places ; he understood
their hopes and their despairs, their sentimentality
and their cynicism. He was the advocate of the
war to end war ; he was the politician to end
politicians. *Il faut en finir* was Clemenceau's
phrase. As President of the Senate Commission
on the Army, a parliamentary body with a watching brief over the conduct of the war, he made
endless tours of the front line, where he was the
terror of dilatory officers and the hero of fighting
soldiers who had never before seen a politician
in such exposed places.

Clemenceau's contribution to *moral* was beyond
all doubt, but his contributions to strategy were
more questionable. Joffre followed the victory
of the Marne not by a further direct attack, but
by a race to the sea in an attempt to turn the
German flank. This failed, although the
Germans' hope of a similar flanking movement
was checked by the British at Ypres. At the end
of 1914 the lines were stabilized and a war of
attrition began. Joffre was convinced that he
could break the German lines. His right-hand
man, Foch, was equally optimistic, but insisted
on different methods : nothing could be done
without artillery ; France must have more 75's,
more 155's. Clemenceau recognized that Joffre
was a good general, but he believed that Foch
was a better—Foch whom, for all his Catholic
faith and his Jesuit brother, he had made head
of the Staff College back in 1909. The refrain of

the *Homme enchaîné* in 1915 was *Les Boches sont à Noyon*, meaning that that fortress must be reduced by heavy artillery before a break-through in the West could be successful, and that all diversionary campaigns must be avoided. Clemenceau poured contempt on Churchill's Gallipoli venture and on the men who had authorized the Salonika expedition and had sent General Sarrail, that good Radical Republican, to lead it.

In 1916 the Boches were still at Noyon. Indeed, they seemed in an impregnable position from Ostend to Baghdad. Joffre's plan for a summer offensive was to attack in force, in conjunction with the British army, on a narrow sector on the Somme. The Germans, however, forestalled him by launching a great attack on the French fortress of Verdun at the end of February. The grimmest months in French military history followed. Joffre sent Pétain with orders to hold Verdun at all cost. Verdun was held, at the cost of 350,000 French lives. Pétain emerged with an unassailable reputation—but for him, Verdun would have been lost and the toll of casualties vastly greater—yet the French armies were crippled, and when the time for the long-prepared Somme offensive came, the English had to make the major contribution. It cost 410,000 British casualties and won nothing but a few useless miles of territory.

The only positive success won by the French in 1916 was a counter-attack led by General Nivelle in the Verdun sector after the main battle was over. The politicians were so surprised and delighted by this that they appointed Nivelle in Joffre's place as Commander-in-Chief. Lloyd George did as much as anyone to engineer the appointment and endorsed Nivelle's plans for an all-out offensive on the Aisne. Nivelle, however, had no qualities beyond self-confidence, and his attack, ill-conceived, ill-prepared and ill-concealed, was such a failure that mutiny broke out here and there among the French troops.

This was the second critical moment of the war for France. It might have been the end if Clemenceau had not stepped in to rally *moral* and Pétain to steady the army. Pétain, now Commander-in-Chief, took a lenient view of the mutinies. He realized that the men had not rebelled, had not refused to obey orders to move into the front line, but had merely declined to go over the top again on Nivelle's orders. He set himself steadily to remove grievances and to restore confidence. By improving the rations, quarters and general conditions of the French soldiers, by refusing Haig's requests for support and leaving the British to bear the brunt of the 1917 fighting at Passchendaele, he gradually nursed the French army back to health. Meanwhile Clemenceau was unshakable in his faith in France and in belief in victory. He was as scornful of the Government's pessimism as he had been of the crazy optimism of Nivelle and Mangin. He had few illusions about the strength of France's allies, but neither did he exaggerate their weakness. England was within a few months of the end of her food supplies, but German submarines could not keep up that pressure for much longer. Russia was in revolution, but the Provisional Government which had replaced the Tsar in March 1917 was at least a government of resistance, committed to offensive war.

He firmly believed that he could win the war for France. At first nobody in high places shared his belief, except possibly the German commanders, who were muttering : " Clemenceau is France's last card." But as 1917 wore on and disasters multiplied, culminating in the dissolution of the Russian front and in the Italian collapse at Caporetto in October, the time came when Poincaré could indeed add : " Now that everything seems to be lost, he alone is capable of saving everything." On November 17th, overcoming his fear of the Tiger who had said that he had " the soul of a rabbit in the skin of a drum," Poincaré called on Clemenceau to form a Ministry.

Clemenceau, who had been waiting for the call, accepted at once and from that moment there was no other power in France. His Cabinet was a gaggle of nonentities—Pichon, Pams, Klotz, Leygues, Claveilles—" the geese," as he amiably explained, " who saved the Capitol." The War

Ministry he kept for himself. It would have been convenient to have had a Socialist in the Government, and Albert Thomas was offered a place, but Thomas refused and Clemenceau was not unduly distressed. He would have liked to have had André Tardieu by his side, but Tardieu was irreplaceable as High Commissioner in the United States. His real colleagues were not his ministers, but members of his personal staff, especially Georges Mandel, who knew everybody, and General Mordacq, who knew everything about the Army.

The British Minister of Munitions, Winston Churchill, happened to be in the Chamber when Clemenceau presented his new Ministry to the deputies ; later he described the scene in *Great Contemporaries*. " Clemenceau . . . ranged from one side of the tribune to another, without a note or book of reference or scrap of paper, barking out sharp, staccato sentences as the thought broke upon his mind. He looked like a wild animal pacing to and fro behind bars, growling and glaring ; and all around him was an assembly which would have done anything to avoid having him there, but having put him there, felt they must obey. Indeed, it was not a matter of words or reasoning. Elemental passions congealed by suffering, dire perils close and drawing nearer, awful lassitude and deep forebodings, disciplined the audience. The last desperate stroke had to be played. France had resolved to unbar the cage and let her tiger loose upon all foes, beyond the trenches or in her midst."

Once he had his vote of confidence a strange serenity came over Clemenceau. It was the calm of an officer who comes on the bridge to keep his watch in a fog, after hours of agonized fretting in his cabin below. It was the sense of fulfilment experienced by a man who had felt frustrated all his life and had been living only for that moment. All observers noted the change in him. " It can be said that he astonished everyone by his patience," wrote Treich. " One expected to find in the Premier the old bitter journalist's impetuosity. On the contrary. Sitting quietly on the front bench, he heard all the speeches without interrupting, his head down, eyes half-closed, not replying to any attack." It was at once the state of a man fulfilled and a man possessed, " that strange state," as Léon Daudet said in his vulgar way, " which comes to the great leader at the height of his success, the great lover in full possession of the object of his love, the great scholar when he reaches the goal of his researches and the great poet when he achieves his master-piece. This state lays a man of action open to every kind of trial and attack and—in the real sense of the word—disarms him. Clemenceau fell into a sort of trance, a state bordering on ecstasy, in which he was to remain, with ups and downs, until the war was nearing its end. . . . His remarkable, inexhaustible vitality, his abstract

172

and concrete love of his country, of his little
Vendée, of his parents and of his old friends, his
sense of the greatness and of the true nature of
the little man, of all the men who were giving
their lives for an ideal which had its roots deep
within them but which had given them nothing
but their labour on the land, their language and
a few noisy days of holiday—all this merged into
a state of ecstasy."

Though Clemenceau was translated, all his
faculties were under perfect control. If he
allowed himself jokes, they were unbarbed :
" The right to slander members of the Government," he declared, remembering *L'Homme libre*,
" shall be beyond all restriction." He worked
to a steady routine, husbanding his strength.
Getting up between five and six o'clock, he would
work in his study in the rue Franklin until the
gymnastic instructor called to put him through
his physical drill. At 8.45 he would be at the
War Ministry, going over the telegrams with
Mordacq. At 9.30 he would see Pichon, the
Foreign Minister, or Philippe Berthelot, " whose
mind," Daudet tells us, " interested him as did
his literary taste, but whom he secretly distrusted." Then Mandel would come to tell him
the news of the day—which was highly necessary,
for Clemenceau never looked at a newspaper.
Later there would be a Supreme War Council,
or a Cabinet meeting, after which Clemenceau
would go home for lunch. By 2.30 he was back

at the office receiving visits until the time came
to go to the House or the Senate.   At 6 he would
go through his letters, interview ministers, talk
with Mandel and Mordacq until 9 o'clock, and
then home to a light dinner and so to bed.   The
only break in this routine was made by visits to
the front—fortnightly and, later, weekly visits to
the battle zones, where the sturdy old man in his
dark tweed coat and battered felt hat became a
symbolic figure, a walking promise of victory.

" There is only one single, simple duty : to be
with the soldier, to live, suffer and fight with
him," he told the Chamber on November 19th.
And later he would repeat : " Home policy ?
I wage war ! Foreign policy ? I wage war ! "
On the home front waging war meant recalling
elderly generals from the front line, finding new
men for the ministries, bringing Sarrail back
from Salonika, sending Nivelle to Algiers and
keeping Lyautey in Morocco.   It meant a purge
of defeatists and collaborationists : Malvy, who
had kept his place as Minister of the Interior until
August 31st, was put on trial for treason ;
Caillaux, who had been in touch with enemy
agents, was arrested on a charge of complicity ;
Bolo Pasha, Mata Hari and other less decorative
spies were executed.   Clemenceau had always
opposed capital punishment, but now—" *Je fais
la guerre !* "

Waging war in foreign policy was not so
simple.   The Russians were about to open

negotiations with Germany. The situation at Salonika was precarious. Italy had not recovered from her defeat at Caporetto. On the all-important Western Front, the Americans were not ready—they had only 150,000 men in France —and the British had failed before Cambrai. Everything depended on increasing the number of effective troops and on getting the Allies to work as a single unit on the Western Front in time to meet the German spring offensive.

These two points were an obsession with Clemenceau. Within a few days of taking office he tackled Pershing, Sir Henry Wilson and Lord Milner on the question of effectives, but the American was doubtful whether the shipment and training of his troops could be speeded up, and the others insisted that Britain was nearing the end of her resources of man-power. There was an agitation in Paris for an immediate offensive, with outcries against Pétain, *le temporisateur*, but Clemenceau knew that Pétain was right. With 175 Allied divisions against 200 German divisions on the Western Front, there could be no question of taking the offensive early in 1918. The utmost the Allies could hope for was to hold the German onslaught.

This was launched on March 21st, on the Amiens sector, where General Gough's Fifth Army was pushed back thirty miles and a wedge driven between the French and the English forces on the Somme. Clemenceau ordered preparations to be made secretly for the Government to leave Paris for Tours. On a visit to Headquarters he found Pétain pessimistic. "After an interview like that," he confided to Mordacq on the way back to Paris in the car, " one needs to have a brass-bound spirit if one is still to have confidence."

If the German success proved anything, it proved the need for a united command. As early as December 1917 Clemenceau had had Foch in mind for the post of Commander-in-Chief. Milner's idea was that Clemenceau himself should become nominal Generalissimo, with Foch as chief counsellor. At a meeting of generals and War Ministers at Doullens on March 18th, at the height of the German offensive, Clemenceau secured agreement on the formula: "General Foch is charged by the French and British Governments with the co-ordination of the action of the inter-allied armies on the Western Front." This was something, but not enough. Soon Foch was complaining that he had to persuade Haig and Pershing instead of commanding. It was necessary to find a firmer formula, and Mordacq suggested that Foch should be given " the strategic control of operations." This was adopted at an inter-allied council held at Beauvais on April 3rd. But it was not for another ten days that Foch was granted the title of Commander-in-Chief of the Allied Armies. Clemenceau's old dream of a united command was achieved at last. Whatever friction there might be in practice, its value in *moral* was to be beyond doubt.

Meanwhile Ludendorff had admitted that his first offensive, against Amiens, had fallen short of its objective. On April 9th he launched his second offensive, in Flanders, when he broke through the Portuguese sector and threatened to drive the English back to the coast. Haig gave his famous " backs to the wall order," and the attack was held at Kemmel Hill. But there was a black month to follow. Clemenceau had no time and no thought now for anything but the affairs of the Western Front. He was constantly out of Paris—on visits to the Headquarters in the field, to the advanced lines, to the inter-allied Supreme War Council. His great problem was to induce the Americans and British to send reinforcements, and in this he was at last successful. Early in May he got the Americans to agree to send 120,000 troops a month to France ; in mid-May he induced the British to bring their depleted divisions up to full strength.

Foch was thus able to regroup his armies in preparation for the third German attack. He expected it to come on the Somme, but the Germans struck farther south, against the Chemin des Dames, which fell on May 27th. The Germans carried the bridges of the Aisne and reached Château-Thiery, within thirty kilometres of Paris.

This was the fourth great crisis of the war for France. The first was in August 1914 when the Germans had reached the Marne, the second in April 1917 when Nivelle's offensive had been followed by mutinies, the third in March 1918 when Gough's army had been driven back and Amiens threatened. Now, after forty-five months, the Germans were on the Marne again. There was some panic in Paris, where fear took the usual form of a demand for a scapegoat. Foch must go—Foch who had refused to move his strategic reserves, Foch of whom even his most devoted admirer, Henry Wilson, was saying : " It is simply damned nonsense saying that he won't *lâcher un pied*, and then running from the Chemin des Dames to Château-Thiery." But for Clemenceau's support, Foch must surely have been removed from the supreme command. He induced Lloyd George and Orlando to add their signatures to a telegram to President Wilson in which he insisted that " General Foch is conducting the present campaign with consummate skill, and his military judgment inspires us with the greatest confidence." He told the Senate Commission : " We must have confidence in Foch and Pétain, those two great chiefs who complement each other so happily." And in the Chamber of Deputies he said : " If in order to win the approbation of certain persons who judge in rash haste, I must abandon chiefs who have deserved well of their country, that is a piece of

178

contemptible baseness of which I am incapable, and it must not be expected of me. . . . Victory is yours if you are calm, confident in yourselves, resolved to see this hard battle through to the end. . . . Do you imagine that it is possible to fight a war in which one never gives ground? There is only one thing that matters : that is the final success, the last victory."

More than at any time in her history, France in those days depended on the will-power of one man. " I will fight before Paris, I will fight in Paris, I will fight behind Paris ; we shall be victorious if the public authorities are up to their task." Clemenceau was no optimist ; it was simply that his mind could not contemplate capitulation. "The Germans may take Paris," he told Mordacq, " but that will not prevent me from going on with the war. We will fight on the Loire, we will fight on the Garonne, we will fight even on the Pyrennees. And if at last we are driven off the Pyrennces, we will continue the war at sea. But as for asking for peace, never ! They had better not count on me for that."

The best comment on this crisis was the cartoon showing a soldier crouching in a shell-hole under bombardment and saying: " *Pourvu que les civils tiennent* "—" If only the civilians can take it."

Clemenceau's confidence in the military chiefs was justified by the events that followed. By the second week in June, Foch and Pétain were ready to go over to the offensive, which they conceived as a series of counter-attacks on separate sectors, intended to prevent Ludendorff from concentrating his armies and to free the lateral railway-lines behind the Allied fronts. They knew that Ludendorff had another shot in his locker, but they shrewdly suspected that it might be his last. On July 15th Ludendorff attacked near Rheims. " The surprise," as the Crown Prince admitted, " failed." Three days later Foch sent Mangin in to launch the first French counter-attack, near Soissons. This was the first obvious success for the generalissimo who in three months of supreme command had had an external record of unrelieved failure. By August 8th the Allied armies were ready for the serial offensive (it was not intended for a knock-out blow but for a succession of stabs which would leave the Germans shaken and the Allies established in favourable positions for the final offensive in the spring of 1919). First the French attacked in the centre, then the British took up the running and forced the Germans back to the Somme. The counter-offensive gathered weight, Foch striking now at the Germans' right, now at their left, now at their extreme right, until the climax came on September 29th, when, on the same day that Bulgaria sued for armistice in the East, the British and Americans broke through the Hindenburg line.

At this point Ludendorff lost his nerve. Even the unshakable Hindenburg admitted that " the gravity of the situation admits of no delay . . . a peace offer to our enemies must be sent at once." On the insistence of the High Command, the new German Chancellor, Prince Max of Baden, telegraphed an appeal to President Wilson for an armistice. Wilson received the telegram on October 6th. It read as follows :

"The German Government requests the President of the United States of America to take steps for the restoration of peace, to notify all belligerents of this request, and to invite them to delegate plenipotentiaries for the purpose of taking measures to avoid further bloodshed.

"It accepts the programme set forth by the President of the United States in his message to Congress of January 8th, and in his subsequent pronouncements, particularly in his address of September 27th. The German Government request the President of the United States to bring about the immediate conclusion of a general armistice on land, on water and in the air."

To Clemenceau this savoured of a trap. Ludendorff was playing for time in which to withdraw his armies to stronger defensive positions whence he would be able to continue the fight with the advantage of interior lines. The emphasis on the Fourteen Points was an attempt to flatter Wilson into trusting Germany and committing the Allies to armistice terms such as would leave her territory and fighting forces intact.

Lloyd George agreed that somehow Wilson's heart must be hardened, somehow negotiations must be taken out of his hands. At a meeting of Allied Prime Ministers in the second week of October, Clemenceau insisted that Wilson be told that an armistice was a military convention, on the drafting of which the commanders in the field should be consulted.

Weeks of feverish inter-allied negotiations followed, while the death-roll continued to mount on the Western Front. Among the military leaders opinions differed. Foch demanded that the armistice should oblige the Germans to evacuate the Rhineland, and Pétain agreed, adding that they should be forced to agree to a huge indemnity. Haig complained that they would never accept such terms ; all one could ask was that they should evacuate the occupied territories and perhaps Alsace-Lorraine. Pershing took the opposite line, that the armistice should be deferred until the Allied troops had reached Berlin ; unconditional surrender was his policy. Clemenceau welcomed these differences. They made it seem that the French commanders were taking the middle way. An armistice in his view did not mean a mere suspension of hostilities, but an instrument to provide the victors with the means of enforcing their final peace-aims. This was also the view of Foch, who wrote to Clemenceau on October 16th ; " It is certain that the armistice should give us full guarantees for obtaining

182

in the course of the peace negotiations the terms which we wish to impose on Germany, and it is evident that the only sure guarantees will be those advantages obtained in the armistice ; that the safeguards in the matter of territory to which the enemy agrees at the time of signing the armistice will alone remain definite."

The question therefore was : What final peace terms did the Allies wish to impose ? Here the crux was the interpretation of the Fourteen Points. If armistice was to foreshadow a settlement based on Wilson's Points, it was essential that the victors should be in agreement on their meaning. On October 29th, at a meeting of British, French and Italian Ministers with Wilson's personal representative, Colonel House, Clemenceau turned to Lloyd George and said : " Have you ever been asked by the President whether you accept the Fourteen Points ? I have not been asked." Lloyd George replied that he had not been asked either. " Then," said Clemenceau, folding his gloved hands, " I want to hear those points."

House read them out, together with the supplementary pronouncements, twenty-seven points in all. Clemenceau and Lloyd George had, of course, known all about them since they were first proclaimed—Clemenceau used to refer scathingly to the President's Fourteen Commandments, adding that " the Good Lord had only ten "—but they had refrained from

183

official comment for fear of weakening Allied solidarity.

Now they raised such acute objections that House threatened that Wilson " would have no alternative but to tell the enemy that his conditions were not accepted by his Allies. The question would then arise whether America would not have to take up these questions direct with Germany and Austria." " That would amount to a separate peace between the United States and the Central Powers ? " Clemenceau asked. House replied grimly : " It might come to that." Clemenceau had to give way. In the end the Premiers agreed to all twenty-seven points, with the exception of that concerning Freedom of the Seas on which Lloyd George refused to commit Great Britain, and with the stipulation that the point referring to indemnities should be amended to cover " compensation by Germany for all damages done to the civilian population of the Allies and to their property." Wilson cabled his acceptance of the amendments, and on November 4th the armistice terms were drawn up. They followed the lines of Foch's original draft which Haig had found too severe. The Allies were to occupy the Rhineland ; the Germans were to surrender their fleet ; the blockade would be maintained.

Even now, when all Germany's allies had collapsed and the Austrian Emperor had signed an armistice which, in Clemenceau's words,

" left him nothing but his breeches," there was a fear that Germany would refuse to sign and that the war would be prolonged into 1919. Foch, asked on October 29th how long it would take to drive the Germans across the Rhine if they refused the armistice terms, replied : " Maybe three, maybe four or five months. Who knows ? " The German delegates sent by the Imperial Government of Prince Max to receive the terms found themselves overtaken by the revolution of November 9th which swept away the Chancellor, the Kaiser and the whole Imperial structure. There was doubt whether the new Government would recognize the delegates or empower them to accept the terms. The signing of the armistice on November 11th came as a surprise as well as an unparalleled relief to France.

All was over bar the shouting. In the evening of the unforgettable day a great crowd gathered in front of the War Ministry in the rue St. Dominique shouting, " Clemenceau ! Clemenceau ! " At last the window opened and the old man appeared. " *Vive la France !* " he said, " *Vive la France !* " It was a sort of apotheosis for Clemenceau. When he and Foch went to London a few weeks later they were greeted as the men who won the war. Lloyd George says of their reception that " it was such as I have never seen accorded to any foreign visitor. . . . The intensity of the enthusiasm was beyond any-

185

thing I have ever witnessed." But Clemenceau remembered the words which Foch had spoken when formally delivering the signed armistice-document to him on November 11th : " My work is finished," said Foch, " your work begins."

Chapter Nine

The Making of a Peace

NOT for a moment did it occur to Clemenceau to resign or even to delegate any of his power after the Armistice. Victory, as he well knew, settles nothing ; at most it creates a situation in which certain things may be settled. His country would have as much need of him during the coming year as she had had during the last : perhaps more. He spent the whole of November 12th at work in his office, giving instructions to his ministers for preparing the Peace Conference.

Clemenceau's view of the cause of war was perfectly simple : German aggressiveness was the cause. His view of the cure was equally simple : Germany must be made incapable of further aggression. The method of securing German incapacity must be to establish strategic frontiers, military alliances and the permanent disarmament of Germany. The problem, therefore, was how to get treaties embodying these means drafted and accepted. Clemenceau realized that this would involve three struggles : first, to get the Allied and Associated Powers to agree on a draft ; second, to get the Germans and their ex-allies to sign ; third, to get the parliaments

187

of France, Britain and the United States to ratify
and implement the treaties.

The state of public opinion in the victorious
countries left Clemenceau with no illusions about
the simplicity of the task of peacemaking. " Yes,
we have won the war," he said to Mordacq,
" and not without difficulty. But now we have
got to win the peace, and it may well be more
difficult still." There was an unreconcilable and
unconscious contradiction in the mind of the
man-in-the-street on whose consent and support
the success of the settlement would ultimately
depend. On one plane of his mind the ordinary
man wanted a peace based on a moral ideal, a
peace that would make not only a safer world
but a better world, a peace founded on what came
to be called Wilsonism. On another plane, he
refused to make any of the sacrifices which the
acceptance of Wilsonism would involve, and
insisted on the victor's pound of flesh. At the
same time that they were crying aloud for
Wilsonism, the Japanese wanted Shantung, the
Italians wanted the control of the Adriatic and
the Brenner, the small nations wanted boundaries
stretching far beyond their natural frontiers, the
British wanted German colonies and shipping,
the French wanted the Rhineland, and the
Americans wanted to keep out of entangling
alliances.

The first problem for statesmen was to decide
which of these two planes—the sacred or the

profane aspect of peacemaking—would emerge uppermost in the minds of men in the years to come. The American President naturally had no doubt that it would be the former ; he disregarded the evidence of the Congress Elections of November 1918 which returned a majority of the isolationist Republican Party. The British Premier tended to agree with Wilson, although the General Election of December 1918 was won on slogans of " Hang the Kaiser " and " Make Germany Pay," and returned many more Conservatives than Liberals to support his coalition Government. Clemenceau, on the other hand, was quite certain that it would be the latter. On December 29th he told the House of Deputies in an impromptu speech just before the parliamentary recess : " There was an old system which seems condemned to-day and to which I do not hesitate to say that I remain to some extent faithful : nations organized their defence. It was very prosaic. They tried to have strong frontiers. They went armed. . . . I was saying that there was this old system of strong and well-defined frontiers, armaments, and what is called the balance of power. . . . This system seems condemned to-day by very high authorities. Yet I believe that if this balance, which has been spontaneously produced during the war, had existed earlier : if, for example, England, America, France and Italy had agreed in saying that whoever attacked one of them had attacked

189

the whole world, this war would never have taken place." He went on to warn the deputies that France could not make peace, any more than she could make war, alone. England and America had been, and would be, essential partners of France. They would have their own ideas of a settlement. "At the Conference, each will defend its interests."

From the beginning Clemenceau kept all arrangements in his own hands. Since the Supreme War Council (transformed overnight into the Supreme Peace Council) had decided that the Conference would be held in Paris, it was certain that Clemenceau would be chairman . . . unless Poincaré should so far forget his constitutional position as to insist on taking part in the negotiations. Clemenceau took pains to remind the President of his constitutional position. As leader of the French delegation to the Conference, it was for Clemenceau to nominate his colleagues. Overlooking Briand and Barthou, he chose the ductile Pichon and the amiable Klotz—"the only Jew I have ever met who knows nothing about finance." Overlooking Berthelot, he chose Jules Cambon, the veteran diplomatist whose conduct he had admired in the Casablanca affair. To these he added André Tardieu, whose incomparable talent for mastering and marshalling facts and for rapidly drafting memoranda was to make him Clemenceau's right-hand man throughout.

It was not Clemenceau's fault if the Conference was not adequately prepared for its work before it met on January 18th, 1919. Within three weeks of the signing of armistice he had sent a note to the American Government suggesting detailed and clear-cut plans for the scope and procedure of the Conference. There was to be a preliminary treaty covering all immediate questions, to be worked out by the four Great Powers and imposed on Germany ; this would be followed by a General Congress of all Powers, including neutrals, to decide details and methods of application and questions concerning the future. As Winston Churchill said, " There is no doubt that the French plan was at once logical, practical and speedy. It placed the settlement of all main questions and all procedure definitely in the hands of the four great victorious Powers who had made the chief exertions in the war ; it drew a line between the past and the future ; above all by the ' suspension of all pre-vious special agreements arrived at by some of the Allies only,' it swept away the whole network of secret treaties contracted in the stress of war. It brought together the four authorities who alone could settle everything, and secured for them an absolutely free hand." But for some reason Wilson disliked it. " No doubt," as Churchill added, " the French proposal was injudiciously framed ; in parts it wore an air almost of cynicism. It seemed to treat high ideals as if they were a mere garnish to agreements on sound policy. The President (Wilson) understood that the overstrained European Allies would be above all things anxious for swift settlement ; and that delaying procedure would increase his bargaining power. So no answer was returned either by him or by Mr. Lansing to the French Note of November 29th ; and no notice whatever was taken of the French proposal to sweep away the secret treaties."

Thus when the Conference met no decision had been taken either in its procedure or on its purpose. Were the treaties to be worked out in concert by the delegations of all the twenty-seven Allied and Associated Powers ? Were their deliberations to be public—" open covenants of peace openly arrived at," in the presence of five hundred representatives of the Press of the whole world ? Was their business to draw up a preliminary or a final peace, a preliminary draft to be presented to the Central Powers for further negotiation or a dictated treaty ?

To these questions Clemenceau proved to have very decided answers. Presiding briskly over the babel of the first plenary meeting of the Conference, he took a high-handed attitude towards the smaller Powers, ejaculating, " *Y a-t-il d'objections ? Non ?* . . . *Adopté* "—like a machine gun, as Harold Nicolson noted. At the second plenary meeting he put them in their place in no uncertain terms. " Sir Robert

192

Borden, the chief Canadian delegate, has very amicably reproached the great Powers for having taken decisions into their own hands. Yes, we have taken decisions . . . I make no mystery about it : there is a Conference of the Great Powers which meets in an adjoining room. The five Great Powers (France, Britain, the United States, Italy and Japan) . . . have lost dead and wounded that can be counted in millions, and if we had not the great question of the League of Nations before our eyes, perhaps we would have been led egoistically to consult no one but ourselves. Who can pretend that it would not have been our right ? " In other words, these five Great Powers were to take the decisions and the rest of the Conference was to endorse them. In fact, the plenary Conference met only five times after that, and its deliberations were formal and empty. The draft of the Treaty of Versailles was presented to it only twenty-four hours before it was presented to the Germans.

Clemenceau was undoubtedly right in insisting that the work of peacemaking would never be ended if left to the full Conference, but he could not expect that the small Powers would be pleased with the manner of this decision. He was also right in insisting that no publicity could be given to negotiations. " Open covenants of peace openly arrived at " did not mean that the Press could be present at meetings of the Council of Ten (so called because it consisted of two delegates from each of the Great Powers) or at those of the fifty Technical Commissions. These Commissions would meet *in camera* ; their reports to the Council of Ten would be secret, as would the private meetings of the Ten and those at which they heard the views of delegates of the smaller Powers. Clemenceau was right, but it was not to be expected that in these circumstances the Conference would get a good Press.

On the more important question of the purpose of the Conference—whether it was to draw up terms for discussion with the vanquished at a later General Congress or to draft a dictated peace—no decision was taken at all. Having failed to get Wilson to accept his November plan, Clemenceau never troubled to substitute another. He knew that in the course of time the principal treaty-makers would become both so tired of their labours and so enamoured of their creation that they would find themselves taking his view that it should be a final, dictated peace.

The Conference made a bad start. European questions proved so thorny that the Council of Ten was glad to accept Lloyd George's suggestion that the colonial question should be treated first. Before the end of January the Ten heard the Australian, New Zealand and South African leaders put forward their case for annexing German colonies on grounds of military security and administrative efficiency. Smuts proposed to sugar the pill of annexation by calling the

194

colonies Mandates, to be held under the still unfounded League of Nations by Allied Powers. Those eventually assigned to the Dominions and to Japan would be mandates of a certain class known as " C " which " can but be administered under the laws of the mandatory State as integral portions thereof." Clemenceau was delighted to see the British and Japanese claim their pound of flesh ; the more deeply they committed themselves to annexation, the less they would be able to refuse France's claims when the time came for him to put them forward.

Wilson approached the Council of Ten with the utmost distrust. He was convinced that he had come into a den of thieves, and in order to head the Allies away from their territorial claims he concentrated on his work as chairman of the Commission on the League of Nations. On this, as on most other subjects, Clemenceau had very definite ideas and the first session of the Commission was confronted with a complete draft constitution for the League put forward by Léon Bourgeois on his dictation. It provided for a strong League executive, a League army distributed over all countries and a League General Staff with overriding powers. " Military instructions shall be given to each member State in accordance with rules designed to procure, as far as possible, uniformity in the armament and training of the troops destined to act in concert. The International Body shall be entitled at any

time to require that their member States intro-
duce any alteration into their national systems
of recruiting which the Staff may report to be
necessary." This was altogether too much for
Lloyd George as well as for Wilson. The
President saw the League not as a new military
instrument but as a new ideal. He would have
nothing to do with the French draft. Gradually
the military sanctions behind the proposed
Covenant were whittled down until they vanished
away. When Wilson insisted on inserting a
clause permitting secession and another weakening American obligations under the Covenant in
deference to the Monroe Doctrine, Clemenceau
lost all interest. He would sign the Covenant
but he expected nothing from the League. In
Lloyd George's words : " He had no faith in it,
no hope for it and no charity towards it."

After meeting twice a day for a month the
Council of Ten had settled nothing. Further
delay was inevitable, for on February 14th
Wilson had to leave for Washington for the
opening of Congress. Five days later the whole
Conference was put in jeopardy by an attempt
on Clemenceau's life. His car was slowing down
to turn out of the rue Franklin when a young man
standing on the pavement fired a revolver point-
blank at his back. The bullet went in beneath
the shoulder-blade and lodged in his lung. The
wound was serious : a man of seventy-eight might
have been expected not to recover from it. But

within a fortnight Clemenceau was back in his place in the Council, more determined than ever to see the business through. He had a week before Lloyd George was due back from London and a fortnight before the return of Wilson. He spent the time in preparing the ground for immediate decisions on the three points which seemed most important for France.

The first was Reparations : Germany must be made to pay not only for repairs but for the whole cost of the war. The second was the Saar Basin : the mines and the whole district must be handed over to France permanently. The third was the Rhineland. On this, the most important question, Clemenceau expected to have the most difficulty. The French case was that the whole left bank of the Rhine should be separated from Germany and should constitute an independent State or States, nominally perhaps under the protection of the League, but actually in the control of France. This Rhineland State and a strip stretching fifty kilometres on the right bank of the river should be under the military occupation of the Allies. Historical and economic arguments had been put forward in support of this case, but the main argument was strategic. While Germany held the Rhine she would be in a position for aggression at some future date. A separate Rhineland was necessary for the protection of France and also, as Tardieu said in a memorandum of February 1919, " it is

197

an indispensable protection for the new States which the Allies have called into being to the East and South of Germany. Let us suppose that Germany, controlling the Rhine, should decide to attack the Republic of Poland, or the Republic of Czechoslovakia. Established defensively on the Rhine, she would hold in check, for how long nobody knows, the western nations coming to the rescue of the young Republics, and the latter would be crushed before they could receive aid." French public opinion was almost unanimously behind Clemenceau and Tardieu in this. The American and British delegates, on the other hand, had always opposed the French plan for the Rhineland. To them it savoured of annexation pure and simple. The Rhineland was after all German in race, language, spirit and economy, and, as Lloyd George repeated, " we don't want to create another Alsace-Lorraine." Obviously the Rhineland would be one of the most thorny problems of the whole peace settlement.

On the very day of Wilson's return to Paris, he and Lloyd George met Clemenceau and made a surprising offer. The United States and Great Britain were prepared, they said, to give a joint guarantee to France, undertaking to come to her immediate assistance in the event of unprovoked aggression by Germany in the West at any future date. In return France was expected to drop her demands for the separation and occupation of the Rhineland.

This offer put Clemenceau in an awkward position. The Anglo-American guarantee was just what he had most wanted for France : it would be unthinkable, suicidal, to refuse it. On the other hand, to abandon the plan for separating the Rhineland from Germany and for occupying it with Allied troops would leave Germany potentially dangerous. Clemenceau therefore accepted the Anglo-American offer but refused the conditions attached. France must have the guarantee *and* Rhineland separation *and* military occupation.

For five weeks controversy raged round this point, Wilson and Lloyd George insisting on their conditions, Clemenceau wanting to have his cake and eat it. It was difficult for him to yield, for Foch had insisted from the beginning that a separated and occupied Rhineland was essential for French security, and Foch now had behind him the President of the Republic (Poincaré) and a body of influential politicians. In the end Clemenceau gave up the demand for separation—a concession for which neither Foch, nor Mangin who had been intriguing with disreputable separatists in the Rhineland, ever forgave him. He concentrated all his dialectical forces on getting Wilson and Lloyd George to agree to permanent military occupation. When Lloyd George pretended the British soldiers would refuse to serve abroad in peace-time, he replied that they made no bones about serving in Egypt and

India ; when Lloyd George complained that France was being egotistical, he answered that the British had taken good care to provide for their own security by depriving Germany of her colonies, fleet, mercantile marine and foreign markets. But no argument could prevail against Wilson and Lloyd George when they were united. Military occupation of the Rhineland for a period of fifteen years was the utmost they would concede. Clemenceau accepted this, but with two highly important qualifications which were duly written in to Article 429 of the Treaty. The period might be extended or the occupation be renewed if Germany should fail in her engagements under the Treaty or if the guarantees should be considered insufficient. This latter provision was inserted because the French realized that the American or British parliament might refuse to ratify the Treaties of Guarantee, in which case France should not be left without the means to military security.

Since Wilson's return the Conference had taken a new form. The Council of Ten had been superseded by a Council of Four, Clemenceau, Wilson, Lloyd George and Orlando meeting privately or with a single secretary (Hankey). In fact it was a Council of Three, for the Italian was interested in nothing but Fiume. This triumvirate was a great improvement on the Ten. Instead of making speeches, the members conversed ; instead of procrastinating, they took

200

decisions. All the important provisions of the treaty with Germany were settled by this Council during the seven weeks between March 24th and May 7th. But the tone of the conversations was none the less acrimonious. " How did you get on this morning ? " House asked Clemenceau one day. " Splendidly," was the reply, " we disagreed about everything." At one time or another each of the Four threatened to leave the Conference.

Clemenceau was a formidable figure at these meetings. The best description of his appearance and manner comes in *The Economic Consequences of the Peace*, written in 1919 by his most acute critic, J. M. Keynes. " At the Council of Four he wore a square-tailed coat of very good, thick, black broad-cloth, and on his hands, which were never uncovered, grey suède gloves ; his boots were of thick black leather, very good, but of a country style, and sometimes fastened in front, curiously, by a buckle instead of laces. . . . His walk, his hand and his voice were not lacking in vigour, but he bore, nevertheless, especially after the attempt upon him, the aspect of a very old man conserving his strength for important occasions. He spoke seldom, leaving the initial statement of the French case to his ministers or officials ; he closed his eyes and sat back in his chair with an impassive face of parchment, his grey-gloved hands clasped in front of him. A short sentence, decisive and cynical, was generally sufficient, an unqualified abandonment of his ministers, whose face would not be saved, or a display of obstinacy reinforced by a few words in a piquantly delivered English. But speech and passion were not lacking when they were wanted, and the sudden outburst of words, often followed by a deep fit of coughing from the chest, produced their impression by force or surprise rather than by persuasion."

More difficult to describe is the impact of his personality. Riddell, the Press chief, not usually an acute observer, had a significant remark in his *Intimate Diary*. " He gives a curious feeling of mental and physical activity. He makes one think and act more quickly." Lloyd George found him personally sympathetic but unapproachable. " I have a difficulty in dealing with Clemenceau. He never goes out to lunch or dinner, so that I must always make a formal appointment with him. That has its disadvantages. If you meet for social purposes, you can raise a point. If you find you are progressing satisfactorily, you can proceed, otherwise you can drop it. Much business can be done in that manner. Clemenceau has no associate with whom I can talk. He treats Pichon as if he were his clerk or manager. Pichon is frightened to death of the old boy, who is certainly a terrifying figure."

A great French journalist was justified in calling the Conference *Le Combat des Trois*. What is not justified is the view that Clemenceau had things all his own way. On March 26th Lloyd George precipitated a crisis by submitting a memorandum urging a lenient treaty with Germany. Clemenceau got Tardieu to draft a biting reply, the gist of which was, in the words of W. M. Jordan, that he " could not follow Lloyd George in his reversal of the Beatitudes. He felt that the British Premier, having first secured for his land an inheritance on earth, now hungered and thirsted rather late after righteousness." On April 7th another crisis was threatened by the news that Wilson had cabled inquiring when his ship could be ready to take him back to America.

Again and again Clemenceau had to compromise. As he had given ground over the Rhineland, so he gave ground over the Saar. The French case was that France should annex that part of the Saarland which had been hers in 1814, that an international régime should control the mining district to the north of this, and that the mines in both parts should become French property. Wilson began by refusing these demands outright. Lloyd George refused the first—annexation—but was prepared to discuss the other two. The eventual compromise provided for political government of the whole Saarland by a League of Nations Commission for a period of fifteen years, after which a plebiscite would be held ; the mines, whose coal was so essential to the French iron-founders of Lorraine, were given to France in perpetuity. It was not the settlement that Clemenceau desired, but it might have been worse. Lloyd George was at his most persuasive : " I am certain," he told Clemenceau, " that if there is a plebiscite, this people will not ask to return to Germany." Clemenceau answered by a sceptical silence.

On the reparations question discussion was more embittered. Clemenceau's view was that Germany should be held responsible for the whole cost of the war. Wilson had opposed this in his Fourteen Points, where he had stipulated that there should be " no indemnities," but he had accepted in October 1918 the qualification that there should be " compensation by Germany for all damage done to the civilian population of the Allies and to their property." The first task, therefore, was to assess these damages. Clemenceau let his ministers fix a fantastic value on damaged French property and insisted that " damage done to the civilian population " should include the cost of pensions for widows and other bereaved persons. The Americans and British countered by demanding an assessment based on German's immediate capacity to pay, citing in support of their proposal the reparations imposed by Bismarck on France in 1871. Clemenceau preferred an assessment based on Germany's future capacity and proposed that the Reparations Commission should take thirty years to collect the sum due. In the end no total sum was fixed. It was agreed that Germany should make certain initial payments at a rate considerably below the original French demands, and that the Reparations Commission should be left to assess the final claim and to determine the manner and date of its payment. With this compromise each of the Big Three seemed satisfied, Wilson because he looked to the League of Nations to temper the wind to the shorn German lamb, Lloyd George because he felt that business men would see that the Reparations Commission acted in a businesslike and not in a punitive manner, and Clemenceau because he knew that League revision could not be made without French consent and that French representatives on the Reparations Commission would not put business before the pleasure of despoiling Germany.

At last the Treaty was ready. The date originally set for the presentation of the terms to the Germans was May 1st, and on April 29th the delegates of the Weimar Republic arrived at Versailles. But in spite of acceleration of business to breakneck speed by the Three and in spite of wonderfully rapid drafting by Tardieu, it was May 6th before the voluminous treaty was finished. On that day it was presented to the lesser States in plenary Conference. They had no time to discuss it, for on May 7th it was formally handed to Count Brockdorff-Rantzau, the German Foreign Minister, at Versailles.

205

The second phase of peacemaking now began. The Allied and Associated Powers had agreed on the terms to be offered to Germany ; the question now was to secure Germany's agreement. Clemenceau expected trouble from the Germans : he was not surprised at Brockdorff-Rantzau's impenitent attitude at Versailles or at the formal German objections to the Treaty which arrived on May 29th and ran to 443 pages. But he did not expect further trouble from the Allies, and he was vastly surprised at the attitude now taken by Lloyd George. The British Premier, impressed by the justice of many of the Germans' objections and terrified lest they should refuse to sign, wanted to modify the Treaty. If the terms were really unjust, the Treaty could bring no lasting peace ; if the Germans should refuse to sign, it would mean the renewal of war. Lloyd George therefore supported the German claims for a mitigation of the reparations clauses, for a revision of the Rhineland and Saarland settlements, and for a redrafting of the provisions made for Silesia so as not to give the German mines to Poland.

Clemenceau must now fight his hardest battle of the year to hold Lloyd George to the decisions he had taken in the council chamber. The Premier had given his consent to the Treaty : how could he dream of going back on it at German instigation ? The Germans would surely sign : if not, the Allies had the means of making them. " We know the Germans better than you do," he told Lloyd George. " Concessions will only encourage their resistance, besides depriving our people of their right. If the Germans know that the Treaty is a peace imposed by the strong who have justice on their side on the weak who were aggressors in their day of strength, they will resign themselves to it. Otherwise they will use our concessions to demand further concessions." Lloyd George was obstinate, and Clemenceau found himself near the end of his strength ; during the early June weeks, for the first time in his life, he was unable to sleep naturally. Gradually, however, Clemenceau, supported for once by Wilson who, having agreed to the terms, could not bear to think that he had agreed to an injustice, forced Lloyd George to give way. The terms were modified in no essential respect (unless the granting of a plebiscite in Upper Silesia be counted as essential) and on June 28th, in a set-piece in the Galerie des Glaces of the Palace of Versailles, the Treaty with Germany was signed.

Yet it was not the end. Although the main work of the Conference was done, there remained to be drawn up the treaties with Austria, with Hungary, with Bulgaria and with Turkey. Endless work lay ahead for Clemenceau, now near his seventy-eighth year. Throughout the stifling Paris August he must grind at the settlement of Danubia, filing down the frontiers of Austria and

Hungary for the benefit of Czechoslovakia, Yugoslavia and Rumania, those potential allies and clients of France. Throughout September he must struggle with the British over the Near East, a struggle which resolved itself into a regrettable *Kuhhandlung*. The British were determined to have control of Palestine ; Clemenceau agreed on condition that French claims in the Lebanon and northern Syria were recognized. The British were also determined to have Mosul ; Clemenceau had already agreed to this, but now he asked in return for recognition of France's right to Cilicia. (His plan was to build a pipe-line from Mosul through French territory to Alexandretta, and he wanted the northern flank to be secure.) When Lloyd George took a high moral line over Cilicia, pointing out that the population, now that the Armenians had been exterminated, was Turkish, Clemenceau reminded him that his tone had not always been so lofty,[1] and that in any case the Anglo-French agreement of 1916 had granted Cilicia to France. He was furious with Milner for delaying negotiations, and with himself for having given a verbal undertaking over Mosul before getting Britain's promise on Cilicia.

[1] After the armistice with Turkey in October 1918, Lloyd George had reminded Clemenceau that Britain had half a million soldiers on Turkish soil and had incurred hundreds of thousands of casualties, whereas other governments "had only put in a few nigger policemen to see that we did not steal the Holy Sepulchre." The regrettable phrase might have been Clemenceau's.

208

Autumn passed stormily and no settlement was reached.

The greatest difficulty of all still lay ahead. How to get the victorious peoples, or rather their parliaments, to ratify and implement the settlement on which their plenipotentiaries had agreed and which their ex-enemies—with the exception of Turkey—had accepted?

The deputies of the French Chamber, elected in 1914, had never liked Clemenceau. He was a member of the other House and had no party behind him. The Chamber and Poincaré had made him Prime Minister against the openly expressed wishes of the deputies, but the times were so critical that they had given their vote of confidence tamely enough. As soon, however, as the tide of victory turned in France's favour, they became critical. The Left feared Clemenceau's authoritarianism, the Right hated his anti-clericalism, and the Centre was antagonized by his contempt of parliamentary combinations. Leaders of all factions had grievances against him for his brusque and cavalier treatment of themselves. He had negotiated the peace without reference to them and he had not taken a single important party-leader into his delegation. He had been a dictator when parliament had asked for a dictator, during the last year of war, and he had continued as a dictator during the months following the Armistice, when parliament wanted nothing of the sort. On his

209

occasional visits to the Chamber in June 1919 he preached the necessity for unity, for a France united in peace as she had been in war, but the deputies saw nothing in this beyond an attempt of *le Père la Victoire* to keep power in his own hands. If Clemenceau could have appealed to the country as Lloyd George did to Britain in December 1918, there would have been no doubt that he would have had the support of the nation, but the French elections were not due until November 1919, and it would be for the old Chamber to ratify the Treaty.

Debates on the Treaty were prolonged over three months between July and October. Their tenor was that Clemenceau had been far too lenient and that he had surrendered the security of France at the behest of Lloyd George and Wilson. The peace settlement was dubbed *la paix Wilson*, and the old criticism of Anglophile and pro-American tendencies was revived against Clemenceau. He had failed to split Germany up ; he had even failed to secure for France that frontier on the Rhine which Foch, the great hero, had always demanded. His vaunted British and American Pacts of Guarantee were all very well on paper, but what use would they be without definite and detailed military undertakings ? He had surrendered French claims to the Saar, and to Syria (when he had accepted a temporary mandate instead of annexation); he had allowed the French case on Reparations to be watered down by Wilson, and he had given in to Lloyd George and the Germans over Silesia.

In English-speaking countries, where the criticism of Clemenceau has always been that he was unduly harsh and obstinate, it must seem strange that he should have been attacked for leniency and compliance. But attacked he was, and the charges did not come only from the Right ; even the Socialist Albert Thomas called the settlement " a sum-total of insufficiency " and asked how it " could constitute a solid security for the country."

Clemenceau's reply to all this was unanswerable, but none the more acceptable for that. He based his apologia on three grounds. First, he had founded the peace settlement on facts, not on wishful thinking. When deputies asked why Germany had not been split up into its component States, he answered that he would have liked to do so, just as he would have liked to have an English Channel between France and Germany, but the facts were against it. " By one of those contradictions which I need not try to account for because they are acts of Providence, the Germans have moved from extreme particularism to extreme centralization. I can do nothing about it. It is their nature ; they are made that way." They showed their unity of conscience against Napoleon, at Leipzig, and " there is no more profound unity than the unity of conscience ; no human being can do anything against that. Unity, you see, is not a matter of diplomatic protocols ; it is in the heart of men." Secondly, he insisted, as he had always insisted, that France could not make peace, any more than she could make war, without the support of Britain and America. It takes at least two to make a successful peace. The continued alliance with the Anglo-Saxon nations was essential to the security of France. He had yielded to Wilson and Lloyd George only to the extent that concessions were necessary to maintain their alliance.

Finally, peace must be regarded as a continuous creation. The Treaty contained all the instruments needed to give France security if Frenchmen were united in determination to use them. "You must not think," he told the House in June, " that after such an upheaval we are going to bring you pages of writing which one after the other will be voted, approved and ratified by the Chambers, and that that will be the end of it and you will be able to go home, all wrongs in the process of being righted, all precautions taken against a new outbreak and everyone able to say : We have a document, now we can sleep. Nothing of the kind ! The life of mankind is not a life of sleep. Life is a struggle. That struggle you can never avoid. . . . When the Treaty comes before you, a treaty with I don't know how many clauses, dealing with all kinds of questions, you must not forget that those complex provisions will be of value only in accordance with what you do. *The Treaty will be what you make it.* If you go to peace resolutely as you went to war, you will make it of service to mankind. If you waste time . . . you will have given our country a dead thing instead of a thing of life." Again and again he returned to this theme. " The Treaty will have no value except according to the manner in which you decide to make it live," he told the deputies on September 26th. " Let us keep together in a union without qualification, without ulterior political motives. Every people lives on a basis of irreducible unity which makes it a nation. That irreducible basis, for us, is the national interest of France."

The two criticisms which might with justice have been made of Clemenceau's part in the peace settlement were never adequately voiced in France. It would have been true to say that his vision throughout had been too exclusively European. He had thought in terms of the security of France against Germany, oblivious of the fact that a world war needs a world peace. The settlement of the Pacific did not interest him. With the future of the Arab world he was not concerned, except in so far as it should secure France's position in Syria. Even Russia was beyond the pale. Bolsheviks he saw simply as terrorists, and he had little reason to believe that they would be successful terrorists. They had come into power in the same month as he, making their *coup d'état* with the promise to abide by the results of elections to the new Russian Constituent Assembly. When the elections proved them to be in a minority, they broke up the Assembly. They threw over Russia's allies and opened negotiations with Imperial Germany culminating in a treaty which liberated German forces for the western campaigns of 1918. It was natural therefore that Clemenceau should urge the Allies to support anti-Bolshevik forces in Russia in the hope of setting up a government which would make some stand against Germany. But after November 11th, 1918, that policy was out-of-date, and Clemenceau seems to have made little effort to substitute another. The Allies hoped to bring an end to the civil war in Russia by inviting the various parties concerned to meet in conference on Prinkipo Island. When this rather naïve invitation was rejected, they had no policy to fall back on. The Supreme Council could not make up its mind whether to support Kolchak and the other anti-Bolshevik leaders with all the supplies at their disposal, or whether to leave Russia to stew in its own juices. When at last, in June 1919, a decision was taken and Kolchak was offered full support in return for his assurance that democratic institutions would be established in Russia, it was too late ; the Red Army had had time to organize, and the Whites were divided, dispirited and on the verge of defeat. Clemenceau cannot escape blame for

214

THE MAKING OF A PEACE

being ill-informed and half-hearted. Two full years after the November Revolution his policy was still to launch a series of Allied campaigns against Lenin, though he did not trouble to press this on Lloyd George and Wilson but accepted their negative policy of non-recognition. " If the decision rested with me alone," he told the Council of Ten, " I would establish immediately round the Bolsheviks a solid barrage to prevent the contagion from spreading. But the decision does not lie with me alone, and, in the presence of the highest allied authorities, I am bound to accept their views."

The same bored acquiescence marked Clemenceau's attitude towards the problem of Turkey—another country which he could hardly consider as European. When the Rhineland discussions were at their height in the Council of Four, he made no objection to the proposal of Wilson and Lloyd George to allow Greek troops to occupy Smyrna. On May 15th, 1919, twenty thousand Greek soldiers landed in Asia Minor and began a massacre of Turks. " I cannot understand to this day," wrote Winston Churchill in 1929, " how the eminent statesmen in Paris—Wilson, Lloyd George, Clemenceau and Venizelos, whose wisdom, prudence and address had raised them under the severest tests so much above their fellows—could have been betrayed into so rash and fatal a step." Perhaps part of the secret lies in the personality of the Greek Prime Minister, one of the few men who deeply impressed Clemenceau. Back in 1899, on his return from a voyage in the Ægean, the Comtesse de Noailles had asked his impression of Greece. " Well, Madame," he replied, " I am not going to talk to you of the grandeur of the Acropolis, nor do I intend to torture you with a lecture on archæology. I have been to see beautiful and picturesque lands, among them Crete. You will never guess, though, that my most interesting discovery on the island was not an antique object but a living man. I will tell you. A young advocate, a M. Venezuelos—or is his name Venizelos ?— frankly, I can't recall it exactly, but the whole of Europe will speak of him in a few years."

If it is true that Clemenceau concentrated too exclusively on European questions, it is also true that he never saw them in their economic aspect. " No arrangement was made at Paris for restoring the disordered finances of France and Italy, or to adjust the systems of the Old World and the New. The Council of Four paid no attention to these issues," wrote J. M. Keynes in 1919. " It is an extraordinary fact that the fundamental economic problem of a Europe starving and disintegrating before their eyes, was the one question on which it was impossible to arouse the interest of the Four." In Wilson or Lloyd George this was to some extent understandable ; they knew little of the Continent. But for Clemenceau there is no excuse. He knew his Europe. He knew what dragon's teeth grow from the seeds of poverty. Yet he ignored the need for a solid financial, industrial and commercial basis for the political settlement. In this, if in nothing else, he showed his age. He was born in the 1840's when gentlemen were not concerned with finance or trade, when Europe had no railways and was not within sight of being an economic unit. To the economic and social disturbances within France herself he was by no means blind, but he gave little attention to their solution. Beyond pushing through in 1919 the long-delayed law for an Eight-hour Day, he got no further than letting them solve themselves *ambulando*. " I have heard people say during the past weeks," he remarked in the Chamber on September 16th, " that the task is superhuman. Yes, there are difficulties in the social field, difficulties of a financial nature—loans which must be paid off, possible upsets, possible social and political conflicts, a hard road ahead, with a darkening sky and an uncertain outlook. All that is true. But what then ? Do you imagine that this is the first crisis that France has undergone ? . . . Remember the nature of the France that will be, and ask yourselves how you may be able to rouse her from this degrading mood of pessimism by an effort of united labour and for an effort of reconstruction. Come, starting from to-day, without bitterness and without criticism, let us lead the nation to its destiny." One cannot help

217

agreeing with Robert Dell who wrote about this time that " Clemenceau's greatest admirer would not venture to say that he ever grasped even the most elementary data of an economic problem or ever thought it worth while to try to do so ; his attitude towards such problems is purely literary and romantic."

The Treaty of Versailles was duly ratified by the French Parliament in October. It would come into force in January 1920. France had her instrument. But how was she to use it ? Who was to lead her, and towards what destiny ?

Chapter Ten

The Last Crisis

NOW surely was the time for Clemenceau to retire from public life. He was seventy-eight. For two years he had worked as few men have ever worked ; he was sick and tired and had deserved well of his country. Surely he should retire in peace, to the books and leisure that were waiting for him in his little Vendée.

Yet there was the question of the peace—the *création continue*, as he had always called it. If Clemenceau were to resign, his place would be taken by Millerand, a man of limited vision and no extraordinary ability. What unity could Millerand induce in France ? What effort would he be able to extort from the people in their present mood of mixed hedonism and lassitude ? And in foreign affairs, how would he deal with Lloyd George, whose language, literally and metaphorically, he could not speak, and with the Americans who had not yet ratified the Treaty ?

Clemenceau did not resign. Confident that the country was behind him and would excuse him from attending too closely to Party politics, he devoted all his energies to the Peace Conference, which was still in session in Paris. The country was no doubt behind him in so far as it was behind anyone, but elections were pending and it is Party politics that decide elections. Thanks to a law passed in the turmoil of July 1919, France had a new electoral system. Instead of ten old single-member constituencies, the *département* was to be the unit of representation. A group of candidates was to be returned for each, and if any one list of candidates got a majority of the votes polled, that list won all the seats for the *département*. Obviously this gave the advantage to the most disciplined Party-group, and it so happened that in 1919 all the discipline was on the Right. The Right-wing groups and others who agreed with them in putting anti-Germanism and anti-Bolshevism above all other interests, domestic and foreign, united and fought the elections as a Bloc National. Clemenceau hoped to put the Radical Party at the head of the Bloc, but many good Radicals preferred to stay outside ; they were shocked by his flirtations with the Right and upset by his neglect of the Party and by his treatment of its pre-war leaders, Malvy and Caillaux. The Socialists were divided into two increasingly irreconcilable groups over the Russian question : the majority was Communist and ready to accept the discipline of the Fourth International ; the minority could find no successor to Jaurès, who had been murdered on the eve of the war. The elections resulted in a victory for the Bloc National, whose candidates won nearly two-thirds of the seats in the Chamber. The Socialists lost 33 of their 101 seats. What was more surprising, the Radicals lost over a half of theirs. The Chamber was overwhelmingly and openly Conservative, for the first time in the history of the Third Republic.

The elections no doubt reflected the mood of the country in so far as it was anti-German and anti-Bolshevik. But they reflected no other facets, and the *horizon bleu* Chamber grossly over-simplified the public opinion of France. (The Socialists, who lost a third of their seats, had polled 300,000 more votes than in 1914. In one Paris division they did not get a single seat though they won one and a half million votes.) The Sena-torial elections which followed early in the new year were hardly more helpful. They showed a slight swing to the Left, bringing Socialists into the august assembly for the first time, but again the Radicals suffered, losing 16 seats. Clearly it would be a difficult team for any government to drive. Much would depend on the new President, who was due for election in that same month of January 1920.

Ought Clemenceau to stand for the Presidency of the Republic ? His friends urged that it was his duty : the country would demand it. But French Presidents are not chosen by the country ; they are elected by Senators and Deputies in congress, voting by secret ballot. Clemenceau was torn between pride and duty. His pride forbade him to present his candidature openly; he had never solicited any post and could never have recovered from a defeat, which he persisted in thinking possible in this case, in spite of the opinion of his advisers. His sense of duty forbade him to refuse to stand; in the American field, if in no other, his authority would be necessary to the Allied solidarity on which peace depended. In the end he compromised. He would stand because, as he told Mordacq, " the moment has come—and it is high time—to prevent America from backing out. We must restore the relations with America that we had in 1918." But he would not stand openly. He would not put his candidacy forward in final form. His friends might send in his name, but in such a way as would enable him to retract it, should there appear to be any possibility of defeat.

His compromise proved to be fatal, not only to Clemenceau's career but perhaps to the Third Republic itself. On January 16th, at a preliminary vote taken to nominate candidates, 389 votes were cast for Clemenceau and 408 for Deschanel, a foppish gentleman who had been President (Speaker) of the Chamber but had no other claims to the country's confidence. Clemenceau immediately had his candidacy withdrawn, and a few days later resigned his Premiership. Deschanel was duly elected President of the Republic.

This was one of the least forgivable acts of all

French parliaments. Lloyd George used too mild a word in calling Clemenceau's defeat " shabby " and was only half right in ascribing it to " a combination of the malcontent elements who thought that he had given in all along the line to the U.S.A. and Great Britain." Clemenceau fell a martyr not only to the cause of French friendship with Britain and America, but also to his own view of the French Presidency. Since the 1870's his policy had been to " vote for the stupidest " and to keep the Presidency weak, and he could see the irony of his defeat by Deschanel, who turned out to be insane and retired to a mental nursing home within a few months. Millerand succeeded as President of the Republic, and the Premiership, after being held during 1921 by Briand, passed to Poincaré, who was to retain it, except for two years between mid-1924 and mid-1926, until July 1929. " The narrow and vindictive Poincaré," to quote Lloyd George again, " became the real ruler of France instead of the more sagacious and far-sighted Clemenceau."

How far-sighted Clemenceau was can be shown more clearly in the years of his final retirement than at any other time of his life. The most deadly of all crises was facing France, the crisis which, a decade after his death, was to be the death of the Third Republic. The people had fallen away so completely from the 1914 mood of exalted patriotism that they cared for nothing

223

but avoiding taxes, getting soft jobs and having the good time to which they felt themselves entitled after their war effort and their victory. The political parties had forgotten their sacred union to such a point that a majority of the Socialists had fallen under the sway of Moscow and most of the Right-wing groups under the scarcely less patriotic dominion of the iron-founders' and mine-owners' federations. Politicians enjoying national reputations were pursuing small vendettas and large personal ambitions. They were even forgetting the one thing on which at the time of Clemenceau's fall they had seemed so determined—the necessity of applying the Versailles Treaty in its full rigour. A month after Clemenceau resigned, they abandoned the clauses providing for the trial of war-criminals, allowing the Germans to have their way over the Leipzig Trials and the Dutch to have theirs over the ex-Kaiser's domicile. In March and April 1920 they allowed Germany to fall behind in the time-table set for her disarmament. That year saw nothing done about fixing the total sum to be paid in Reparations, and throughout 1921 Germany's schedule of obligations was scaled down.

France was about to lose the peace, and Clemenceau saw it. " We are marching to catastrophe so complete," he wrote to Martet in 1922, " that it is impossible for me to find a way out of it. The worst of it is that these puppets

224

who have brought us to this point are only in part responsible. They have given themselves away. The country has tolerated everything. Even to-day all it can do is to wring its hands. The defeat of Germany was crushing. Yet see how she rebounded. Amongst us I can only see the lowest sort of personal ambition in the midst of complete apathy." He could find no way out of it because he was powerless. A few weeks after resigning office he had gone for a tour in Egypt, and then, after a trip to Java and India, he had settled down at St. Vincent-sur-Jard in the Vendée, where he rented a cottage on the sand-dunes facing the sea. He had no party, no position and no future.

Yet there was one thing he could do, one duty he could perform—the duty that he had had in mind when he had let his friends put forward his name for the Presidency. He could go to America and try to " restore the relations that we had in 1918." This was now more urgent than ever. In November 1919 the United States Senate had refused to ratify the Treaty of Versailles. They had also rejected, by a majority of six, the Pact of Guarantee, the pact which their President had promised and which the British House of Commons had ratified without so much as a debate. America's defection meant the end of the whole guarantee, for Britain was not bound to apply the Pact until it had been ratified by the United States. Then the Americans went further : they signed a separate peace with Germany. No Frenchman now except Clemenceau could have a chance of bringing Americans to a sense of their obligations. He knew that everything had changed since he had spent four years in the States, back in the 1860's, yet there was a sense in which everything was the same. Americans in their hour of victory had turned from the cause for which they had fought, as they had turned from Lincoln's cause after the victory of 1864. Once again they were letting slip an opportunity such as history rarely vouchsafes twice in a lifetime. Yet Clemenceau stood by the prophecy he had made in *Le Temps* in 1865 ; " There will be long flounderings in the void of incomplete, tentative solutions, but this people will always end by seeing where justice and truth lie." He must go to America; it had always been his second country.

On the eve of his departure in 1922 he read in the *New York Times* an interview given by Marshal Foch, who had just returned from an American visit. " Clemenceau," said Foch, " is going over there to whimper and sentimentalize like the old dotard that he is. . . . Clemenceau has lost the peace. His apologia would have little success in France ; he is hoping to have more success with it in the United States. He is going over to say to the Americans : ' You are really very naughty. Why have you not ratified my treaty ? ' . . . If I could give him a bit of advice I would tell him to stay at home ! But he has not asked
226

for my advice. The journey is a piece of personal publicity. It is devoid of any practical value."

That interview spelled failure for Clemenceau's American tour. Personally it was a great success. He visited the national shrines—Springfield, Mount Vernon, Arlington. He made speeches in New York, Boston, Chicago, Saint Louis. He was entertained by President Harding, after his manner. But Americans listened to the Tiger's roar as they would to that of any circus-star, without asking themselves what he had to roar about. It would take more than an octogenarian tiger to shake them from their normalcy.

Clemenceau could never quite get over Foch's ingratitude ; he was to harp on it continually during the years that followed. After all, he had made Foch. He had put him at the head of the *Ecole de Guerre* in 1909, when every political reason was against the appointment ; he had worked unceasingly in 1917 to make him Commander-in-Chief of the Allied Armies, when French soldiers would have preferred Pétain ; he had defended him in May and June 1918, when politicians and publicists were clamouring for his demotion after the affair of the Chemin des Dames. Until October 1918 his relations with Foch had been friendly, almost affectionate. After that there was a rift, widening during the Peace Conference until it became an open breach. Why did the two " co-architects of victory " quarrel so bitterly? They had so much in common—the same deep and narrow patriotism, the same force of character, the same way of living off will-power. Foch identified his country with his religion, Clemenceau identified it with himself; but there was no need for a clash over that. The quarrel came because each insisted on overstepping the dividing line between their professions. Foch in strategy, like Clemenceau in politics, learned to be circumspect, compromising, opportunist; in each other's profession both remained *simpliste*, doctrinaire. The trouble was that neither would recognize a dividing line. " War is too serious a matter to leave to soldiers," Clemenceau repeated. " As for the notion so vociferously proclaimed by M. Pichon and Clemenceau, that a general works on one side of a barrier and diplomatists on the other," Foch replied, " there is nothing more false or, one can even say, more absurd." Clemenceau could never forgive Foch, but he was never unfair to him. " Speaking of Foch," he said to his exsecretary in 1927, " well, Martet, you see how he conducted himself towards me, all the shabby little tricks he played on me, how warily I was forced to walk with him—yet despite all that he was the man we needed. With Pétain, a loyal and trustworthy man, who behaved himself in exemplary fashion, the war would have lasted another year."

Clemenceau's relations with Poincaré were as

strained as his relations with Foch, but here the case was altered. The two men had always disliked each other. Clemenceau never had any sympathy with the formal-mannered, meticulous Lorraine lawyer. He had done his best to prevent Poincaré's election as President of the Republic in 1914, he had attacked his conduct during the first three years of war, had held him at arm's length during the peace negotiations and had manœuvred successfully to prevent his re-election to the Presidency in 1920. The reappearance of Poincaré on the political scene (he held the combined offices of Prime Minister and Foreign Minister between January 1922 and June 1924) disgusted Clemenceau. On the German question Poincaré and Foch saw eye to eye. The difference between them and Clemenceau was that they wanted a Carthaginian peace, whereas Clemenceau wanted a peace that would be Carthaginian only to the point which Britain and America, France's necessary allies, would allow. "The keynote of the Treaty of Versailles," Clemenceau was to write in his last book, with a side-glance at American readers, " is the *liberation of the peoples,* the independence of nationalities, whereas the keynote of the policy of Marshal Foch and M. Poincaré was the *occupation* of territory by force of arms against the will of the inhabitants." And he added a typical Clemenceau sentence : " They had no wish to take anything except from their neighbours ; but that being

conceded, they were peremptory in insisting that
no one must follow their example."

In 1923 the policy of Foch and Poincaré
prevailed ; French and Belgian troops marched
into the Ruhr. The possible necessity for this
occupation had been foreseen by Clemenceau in
his treaty-making days, but he had never envisaged its being carried out without the assent of
Britain and the United States. In the circumstances of 1923 it could be nothing but an irre-
parable blunder. It reduced Germany's capacity
to pay reparations, convinced large sections of the
German people that France was vindictively
determined on their ruin, and did much to swing
British and American opinion from sympathy
with France to sympathy with Germany. In
France the masses soon came to see Poincaré's
policy as a mistake : they had lost the will to
dismember Germany, they disliked having to send
their conscript sons to serve abroad, and they
were bitterly indignant at the new taxes which
Poincaré found it necessary to impose in order
to pay for the Ruhr occupation. The general
elections of 1920 had shown a strong swing to the
Left. The Bloc National was defeated by the
Cartel des Gauches, an electoral union of the
Radical and Socialist parties. Poincaré resigned,
and the Radical Herriot forced the resignation of
Millerand, who had unwisely campaigned for the
Bloc National from the heights of the presidential
palace.

The fall of Poincaré and Millerand was no consolation to the old man who watched France's fortunes so zealously from his cottage on the Biscayan coast. For the next two years the real ruler of France was to be Aristide Briand, whose policy of collaboration with Germany in concert with Britain and America seemed to Clemenceau to be even more noxious than Poincaré's former policy of victimization without concert had been. If Clemenceau could never be really unfair to Foch, he could never begin to be fair to Briand. " Do you think," he had asked when Briand had offered him a seat in his Cabinet in 1915, " that a thoroughbred can go into harness with a toad ? " It was gall to him to see Briand, now at the head of affairs, recalling to office the very men whom he himself had dismissed for treachery or incompetence—Caillaux, Malvy, Sarrail. It was wormwood to hear of his amicabilities to Stresemann, whom Clemenceau believed to be the Junkers' agent, the Prussian of Prussians. Every act of Briand's, every new concession to Germany—over reparations, over admission to the League, over Locarno—seemed to Clemenceau to drive a new nail into the coffin of France.

This view may have been far-sighted, but it was scarcely sagacious. In the situation that followed the disastrous Ruhr occupation there was no alternative to a policy of co-operation with Germany in concert with Britain and America, and no one could say that Briand did not pursue

231

the policy with skill. The weakness of the Cartel des Gauches lay not so much in its foreign as in its domestic policy. Here finance was the crux, and in finance Clemenceau was not interested. The Government could not balance the budget and its supporters were divided between the Socialist panacea of " soaking the rich " by capital levy or increased income tax, and the more conservative solution of retrenchment combined with heavier indirect taxation. Caillaux, who had a more constructive policy, asked for extraordinary powers to enable him to set about thoroughgoing financial reconstruction. The Chamber refused them. Meanwhile panic swelled like a snowball and the value of the franc fell till it reached 250 to the pound sterling. It was a crisis of confidence, calling for an elder statesman with a reputation above Party ties and aims. The only man who could create confidence was Poincaré. His recall to the Premiership in July 1926 ended the crisis and he had no difficulty in stabilizing the franc at 120 to the pound.

To Clemenceau's disgust, Poincaré retained Briand at the Ministry of Foreign Affairs—Briand, whom he believed to be capable of every iniquity, every treachery. " Mark well what I am telling you," Clemenceau said to Martet in September 1927, " in six months, in a year, in five years— when they like and how they like—the Boches will invade us." But he realized that Cassandra never saved a nation. Clemenceau had to act, and two lines of action were still open to him. He could appeal to America and he could appeal to the conscience of France. In the summer of 1926, when his life seemed at its lowest ebb (his friend Monet was blind and dying a cruel death), he spent weeks on drafting an open letter to President Coolidge. " You are demanding from us the payment of debt, not of a commercial debt, but a war debt, and you know just as well as we do that our cash-box is empty. . . . Three mortal years we waited for that American word, ' France is the frontier of freedom.' Three years of blood and money flowing from every pore. Come and read in our villages the unending list of our dead, and let us compare, if you will. Is not the living energy of all that lost youth in itself a ' banking account ' ? "

Then for the appeal to France. Clemenceau set himself to write his last book, *Grandeurs et Misères de la Victoire.* It is the work of a very old man and falls far short of being the history of the great ministry of 1917–19 which Clemenceau alone could have written, yet it is full of fire and polemical brimstone, and as a criticism of the foreign policy of his successors and as a warning of the wrath to come it is unsurpassed. After a long and in the main justified reply to Foch's attacks and a description of the salient points in the Treaty of Versailles, he devotes a hundred pages to what he calls " The Mutilations of the Treaty." Here he calls attention to six major mutilations. First, the American defection and the extraordinary situation produced by the United States which, after refusing to accept the obligations imposed by the Treaty, insisted on taking her full share of the benefits. " The separate peace made by America, who might have been the arbiter of the peace of Europe, has thrown the Continent back into its age-long state of strife by a display of financial greed upon which the future will give its verdict." Secondly, the climb-down over Reparations. Why, in January 1922, was " the President of the Reichstag able to announce that in a space of two years, Germany had procured a reduction of 40 per cent. in the financial obligations imposed on her by the Treaty of Versailles ? " How could France have consented to the Dawes Plan under which " the United States became the arbiters for everything concerned with the execution of one of the most important parts of the Treaty of Versailles *which they had not ratified*? "

Thirdly, the Locarno Treaties which Clemenceau regarded as an abrogation of Versailles and as an insufficient guarantee either to France or to her East European allies. Examining the Locarno texts, he noted that " Germany implicitly declares—and Europe supports her contention—that she does not give up hope of a subsequent modification of her Eastern frontiers." He saw that the anti-militarist clauses of the treaties included the proviso " unless it is a question of exercising the right to legitimate defence," and he commented : " A nation that wants to wage war is always in a state of legitimate defence." Above all, Locarno shocked him by the fact that " all the contracting parties are put on the *same* footing as regards the menace they constitute to peace." Clemenceau could never regard this as anything but a hollow mockery of justice. Germany had been the aggressor in 1864, in 1866, in 1871 and in 1914 ; she would be the aggressor again. Would the lion lie down with the lamb just because it had been admitted to the Genevan fold ?

Fourthly, the question of Disarmament. France, Clemenceau pointed out, had now reduced her period of military service to one year and had raised the retiring age of Generals from sixty to seventy. Germany had been allowed to find ways of training soldiers in rifle clubs and all manner of other para-military organizations, and her Reichswehr, though small, had one trained officer or non-commissioned officer for every three men. " In 1928 France spent six milliards of francs on her armed forces : Germany spent eight milliards." In all this Clemenceau was giving France the warning which Winston Churchill, alone among statesmen, was to give England in later years.

Fifthly, the question of organizing frontier defence. With the peace settlement mutilated by the loss of the Anglo-American guarantee, France had to devise her own methods of defending her frontiers. " From 1920 to 1928 there were two schools of thought in opposition, the Fortified Regions school and the Continuous Lines school. . . . For eight years they have disputed without any result. At last, in 1928, the Fortified Regions school got the upper hand. So it is this system that is to be adopted. Nearly ten years have been lost in futile wrangling. The Fortified Regions system is to be applied solely to that part of the North-Eastern frontier which stretches from Luxembourg to Switzerland. As regards the rest (the Franco-Belgian frontier and the Swiss frontier), we are reckoning on Belgium and Switzerland organizing their German frontiers. Thus the great lesson of 1914 has been of no avail ! " Clemenceau made all the criticisms of " Maginot-mindedness " which were to become commonplaces a decade after the posthumous publication of his book.

Finally, Clemenceau called attention to the mood of the defeatism which was a mutilation of the very spirit of the Treaty. The traitors had been brought back from exile and restored to high places in the Capitol. Briand made Malvy Minister of the Interior again in 1926 ; Caillaux was back too. Clemenceau saw the defeatist mood of France as clearly in 1928 as lesser men were to see it in 1938. He foretold with uncanny accuracy the events which would follow. Successive mutilations of the Treaty would enable

the Germans to put across the view that Versailles
had led to nothing but social disturbance and
recriminations followed by outbreaks of violence.
" That will be the day for which Germany has
been ceaselessly striving since the Treaty of
Versailles. What forces are at the disposal of
the new nations of Central Europe ? What help
will they afford us and what support are we in a
position to offer them ? All the problems raised
by the German aggression of 1914 will have to
be dealt with at one and the same time.
Germany, having regained her strength, will have
inevitably bargained for arrangements from which
her concern to isolate France will not be excluded.

" I pause on the threshold of this terrible
moment when the last great struggle will be
entered upon. Who then shall decide the fate
of historic France, as the fate of Athens was
decided on the day of Chæronea ? The Mace-
donian could do no more than rend asunder the
world that had laid the foundation of civilization.
In the end he gained nothing by it. But his
achievement sufficed to bring about manifold
dispersions of energy, to break and crush those
attempts at a renaissance in which the noblest
effort of man's finest ideal had been engaged."

There was much that Clemenceau did not see,
much that he failed to understand when complet-
ing this book in the eighty-eighth year of his life.
He was still thinking in terms of a world centred on
France, a world in which Germany was the only

aggressor. His ideas for international organization went no farther than defensive alliances for
France, particularly with Britain and the United
States. " The principal discovery we have yet
to make is that *it needs at least two* to maintain an
honest peace." He still ignored Russia, which,
in the first years of his Five-Year Plan, was for
him, as for Winston Churchill, merely the Bolshevik
Bogey, all the more negligible now that it had
failed to stir up revolution in the West. He did
not see that without Russia there could be no
safe bulwark against Germany. He did not see
that economic dislocation was at least as dangerous to the peace of the world as political
dislocation. Problems of finance, commerce
and industry still bored him. His responses were
always those of a man born in the 1840's.

. Yet there was much that a man born in the
1840's could do for the France of the 1920's.
There was the same need for a united Republican
Party that there had been in Gambetta's day.
There was the same need for a check on the
bribing of journalists—as the Hanau scandal
showed—that there had been in the days of
Panama. There was the same need to regard
deputies as the servants of the commonwealth
rather than as the agents of their constituents.
Lord Bryce, writing of the French deputy in 1920,
said : " Every service is expected of him. He
must obtain decorations for his leading supporters
and find a start in life for their sons and sons-in-

law. Minor posts under government and licences to sell tobacco have to be secured for the rank and file. All sorts of commissions to be performed in Paris are expected of him, down to the choice of a wet-nurse or the purchase of an umbrella. . . . Ministers dispense the honours, the medals, the ribands, the administrative posts, mostly of small consequence, the tobacco licences, and even the college bursaries. To them the deputy goes when the commune or the arrondissement desires a bridge or a road, when a farmer wants to be compensated for damage done to his vines by a hail-storm, when a taxpayer disputes the tax-gatherer's claim, when a parent wishes to have an indulgent view taken of his son's performance in an examination, when a litigant thinks that a word of recommendation might help him in a court of justice." This attitude was every whit as dangerous to France now as it had been in the early days of the Republic. The problem on the political plane was how to identify private interests with the national interest, how to identify the nation with the Republican State. There was a task there which Clemenceau might have performed ; but he was too old.

In every respect but one it might be said that Clemenceau had outlived his age, but that one was all-important. He held fast to the view that the greatest social force in the world is Nationalism, and in this he was to be proved right by the events of 1939–45. " I have always been the same," he told the people of Mouilleron-en-Pareds in 1922 : " Life has taught me much, and I have ended by recognizing that some of my ideas should not be given the same importance as before. But I have always recognized that there is nothing higher than the sentiment of national fraternity of all the French people." Nothing higher, and nothing more difficult to galvanize into action in the day-to-day conduct of peace-time life. From the point of view of his limited vision he had seen the essential. No one else in the 1920's felt more acutely the crisis which was upon France, the crisis which was to intensify during the 1930's until it finally engulfed the Republic in *l'an quarante.*

Envoi

CLEMENCEAU lived for nearly ten years after his retirement. They were years o almost complete oblivion. It was known that he had made his home on the Vendéen coast and that he still kept his Paris flat in the Rue Franklin where he spent some winter months, but he was forgotten, a relict of the past, no more noticed though a good deal better preserved than most ancient monuments in France.

At Saint-Vincent-sur-Jard he lived more than modestly. His home was a single-story cottage, pitched low against the Atlantic gales. There were three rooms opening out of each other, a barn which he converted into a library, a strip of sand which he coaxed into a garden. His household consisted of Albert, his old valet, with Madame Albert looking after the kitchen, and the chauffeur Brabant who had always driven his car. There was no guest-room, and the only regular visitors were his daughters, Madame Jacquemaire and Madame Jung, and his son Michel.

He was a very old man, preparing to meet the Maker whom he had always denied in the manner which he had always upheld. His mind turned to ancient Athens : " It's something that has always sustained me. When I was weary of all the imbecilities of which politics is composed, I turned my spirit towards Greece. Others went fishing. To each his own way." He was not a scholar, only an enthusiast. Thinking about Greece meant thinking about Pericles' oration and of the victory that the Athenians had won and thrown away. Soon he was writing about Demosthenes, his hero of heroes. The little book which he published in 1926 was ostensibly a eulogy of Demosthenes, but actually an *apologia pro vita sua*. One hardly knows whether one is reading about Athens or about France, about Demosthenes or about Clemenceau. " He would have saved his country if it had consented to be saved. Athens needed to exert a continuous effort of will if it were to remain independent. It lacked nothing but persistence of will. . . . Nations have never cheerfully followed any leaders except those who have asked them to shed their blood." More than once an observation creeps in which was certainly not inspired by Athens. " Pascal, who divined everything, has pointed out to us that the great of the world are taken out of themselves by the exercise of power, since it turns them away from intro-spection, but that they are *left miserable in their fall because no one keeps them from thinking about themselves.*"

All his life Clemenceau, who had been frightened of nothing else, had been afraid of himself. Fearing to know himself, he refused to let anyone else know him. Very early in life he had adopted a mask which served him successfully to the end. His dark eyes had a hard, impenetrable glaze, and the lips which might have given him away were covered by a heavy moustache. His manner was almost ceaselessly cynical, his tone ironic, his humour brutal and outrageous. The *boutades* and *lazzis* which made up his conversation, the rip-rap of quip and sally, were designed to repel intimacy and to ward off self-knowledge. For in truth, like all " characters," he was a man divided against himself. Fearing to know himself, he could not love ; fearing that others should know him, he could not let himself be loved. When a personal relationship seemed to be approaching the point of a mutual recognition, he would put up the mask, and if the intimacy did not dissolve at once he would cauterize it with mockery. With women he adopted the convenient masculine evasion, keeping his relations on the footing of gallantry and sensuality. With men there was an even simpler evasion : he refused any relationship in which he was not the master. Yet his emotional nature was not starved ; it found a compensatory outlet in generalized affection for children and for soldiers, for the Vendée and for France. Like so many divided natures, he had charm, and the capacity to charm did much to compensate him for the lack of capacity to be loved.

Clemenceau made two exceptions to his refusal to admit friendship. The first was in the case of Gustav Geffroy, a much younger man whom he had first met in the old *Justice* office in 1881. With him the relationship was that of master and disciple, but there was something about the unhappy, introverted Geffroy which made for intimacy. Geffroy's understanding of his master was probably deeper than that of any other man ; he was a sensitive writer, and had he lived we should probably have known more about Clemenceau than we shall ever now be told.

The other exception was Claude Monet. Here the relationship was reversed ; it was Clemenceau who was the disciple. He felt for Monet a sentiment of which he had seemed incapable and which he certainly never felt for anyone else—a sentiment of unmitigated respect. " I've always had a great respect for Monet," he admitted to Martet before hastening to try to explain it away. " In the first place, we lived on two different planes—never collided, never fought. In the second place, he painted exactly as I should have done had I been a painter." There were other grounds for respect. Monet was a wholly integrated, completely single-minded man. He was older than Clemenceau and the only one of all his acquaintances who had survived the allotted span and kept to the work of translating his vision in defiance of old age. Clemenceau

244

admired him and—it is not too much to say—
loved him. It was to Monet in his garden at
Giverny that Clemenceau came in every spare
hour that he could snatch from public affairs
during the war and the Peace Conference, and to
Monet that he turned after his retirement. In
India his one regret was that Monet was not with
him to see Benares—" a vast river, pale blue with
a great curve of white palaces shading away into
the powdery dawn light." At Saint-Vincent-
sur-Jard, the same regret : " If you don't come
too late you'll see the lotuses, though the cows
have eaten at least a third. The sea here fas-
cinates me. I'll try to make you share my joys.
How pleased I am that you can write ' I have
been doing a lot of work.' That speaks volumes.
For my part, I've got nothing done—my hands
are on fire and my right shoulder is in demolition.
But I don't worry when the waves come and
tickle the soles of my feet. I wouldn't be surprised if you got an appetite for painting here.
There are blues and greens on the palette of sky
and sea. There are pictures in it. So come
quickly. *Et puis je vous embrasse.*"

These letters written to Claude Monet in his
eighties are among the most warm-hearted and
least defensive—or least aggressive, it comes to
the same thing—that Clemenceau ever wrote.
One example is worth quoting at greater length ;
it was dated March 1924, when Monet was nearly
blind.

Mon cher vieux maboul,

I really think that I like you best when you are stupid. But in spite of the pleasure of liking you, I wish you weren't stupid quite so often.

You have got a double cataract. These things happen to everyone. You have felt it the more cruelly because you are an artist *hors pair* and you have set out to do with failing sight better work than you did with two good eyes. The admirable thing is that you have succeeded. There lie the elements of your present unhappiness.

. . . But the good Lord will tell you that one can't perform miracles all the time. You are only a man, my friend, and I am glad of it, for if you were the good Lord you would be a great bore. Happy imperfection ! . . . You must rest. . . . That is easier for me to say than for you to do. But you are Monet.

Et puis lavez-vous la tête de ma bénédiction.

G. CLEMENCEAU

In 1926 Monet died, and Geffroy too. Clemenceau was now bitterly lonely but far from broken. He set himself to raise a monument to the memory of the great painter. It took the form of a monograph, *Claude Monet : Les Nymphéas* in the Plon Series on *Nobles vies — Grandes œuvres*. It contains some of Clemenceau's best writing, and makes one realize what the world lost in æsthetic appreciation when the Tiger's passion for action kept his nose to the political trail.

On politics Clemenceau thought little during

his later years. He defended the peace settlement by reflex action and fulfilled his duty in warning France and the world of the catastrophe to come, but on the fundamental problems of politics he had nothing new to say to the generation of the 1920's. Nowhere in his later writings is there any serious contribution towards an answer to the questions which he himself had posed so shrewdly in earlier years—questions of the relations between democracy and demagogy, of the recruitment and promotion of rulers, of the function and limitations of bureaucracy. "Democracy," he had said, "is not demagogy. Democracy does not mean the permanent and unchangeable equality of all individuals. If it did, one would have before one only two solutions to the problem of the State and of government : either anarchy pure and simple, or the election of all government officials by drawing lots. That latter system was practised in Athens, but you know as well as I do that that was for show : the real rulers were not the authorities who had been chosen by lot. . . . No, democracy is essentially the régime in which people are governed by *élites*. Find the best way of forming *élites*— that is the essential problem of democracy. The régime should be such that the *élite* could be drawn from all sections of the nation. . . . Extend the intelligent sections of the upper classes ; infiltrate them by extending the intelligent sections of the lower, so that the rulers will come

247

back to their point of departure and will lead in a direction that may be acceptable to and practicable by the nation as a whole. . . . Whatever a country's form of government may be, it will always end by falling into bureaucracy unless it is dominated by exceptional personalities. What should the administrative body really be? An immense machine for guaranteeing liberty, for allowing liberty to evolve, for achieving social justice, which is *the point where the interests of all citizens meet.*"

But Clemenceau had said all that back in 1910 (in conversations recorded by his secretary Léon Abensour). Later he had nothing to add. " The truth is that we have never been governed except by interested oligarchies, under various names," he wrote in 1926. " In our own day Sovietism and Fascism attest a revolutionary feeling in the common people against the reprehensible practices of ' democratic ' oligarchies. . . . Democracy, long the supreme hope of badly governed peoples, provoked, by its uncontrollable chatter and by the too obvious lowering of character, the violent reactions embodied in Sovietism and in Fascism—not to mention other forms of government which may be in the making. . . . Alas, Fascism and Sovietism are nothing but empirical preparations for the return of the old tyrannies." All of which may have been true, but was hardly a constructive contribution to the solution of problems facing European democracy.

When Martet pressed him in 1927, his reply was impatient and trivial. " What annoys me in the case of France is that all my life I have fought for what they call the freedom of the Press, freedom of speech, *et caetera*. Now I have come to believe that all these freedoms end in the worst form of slavery and degeneration. Before setting the French free, it would have been better to have taught them what freedom is and how to make proper use of it."

In the latter end of his life Clemenceau addressed himself to problems more fundamental than those of politics. Before he could tell how men may live together in freedom, he had to answer the question : What is man ? Before he could die in peace he had to answer the question : What is life ? Being a good Frenchman he must strive to make his answer lucid, logical and, as far as might be, complete. And so Clemenceau, racked by diabetes and hardly able to stand, set to work and wrote his *Summa*.

Au Soir de la pensée is an enormous book—a thousand pages in the regrettable American translation. It is a sort of compendium of materialist philosophy written by an amateur scientist who had studied Lamarck and Darwin in the morning and Rutherford and Perrin in the evening of his thought, and who had lived his high noon in the heat of the science-versus-religion controversy. All the atheist's gibes against Christianity are there, most of the evolutionist's arguments, and

249

many of the humanist's scruples. "Thus, after mythical explanations have failed, scientific research will show us man in the guise no longer of a defective demi-god, but in that of a progressive representation of the evolution of life moving towards the unknown destination which we vainly try to anticipate in our dreams." Clemenceau never stops to define his terms. "All in all," he goes on, "is it not possible for us to remain good children of the earth, without other ambition than that of making the most of ourselves in the terrestrial conditions from which we cannot escape." (Again, no definition : what are our *selves* ?) "To live is the sensation of imaginary permanence amid the elusive wheel of things of which India had a glimpse, only to feel an irresistible temptation to escape from it. . . . The aim of life," he insists, "is to know enough of the world and of yourself to systematize your thoughts, to rule your emotions, honestly to direct your personal actions, and to contribute your just share to the social activities of an harmonious altruism." The reader gets no answer to his clamour for a definition of terms, but Clemenceau seems to feel surprise at the use of the word altruism. "People do not realize clearly enough," he explains, "that an enlightened unselfishness affords a more refined contentment than does the most cleverly disguised self-seeking." He is writing for his own satisfaction rather than for the public (" If I had never written that book

I should feel myself uncomfortable in Eternity "), and has almost forgotten his reader. The only person he stops to argue with is Pascal ; again and again in this book he seems to be conducting with Pascal the same sort of dialogue that Pascal conducted with the " Pyrrhonien " in the Pensées. At the end of the book Clemenceau is left face to face with death. " A dreamless sleep— that is, a purely negative state of unconsciousness —is all that we can anticipate of death. That is not very terrifying."

Au Soir de la pensée was written for the most part in 1926, between the monograph on Demosthenes and that on Monet, but in a sense it was a life's work. The doctoral thesis on the Generation of Anatomic Elements, written more than sixty years earlier, was a preliminary sketch, and the essay on Monet was intended as a prologue to a final volume which was to deal with the emotional impulses as expressed in . art and religion—a volume that never got written, which is perhaps just as well. *Au Soir* did not have a favourable reception; even Mordacq could say no more than that " it was received with deference, but did not arouse any very great enthusiasm." Yet the very absence of enthusiasm is significant. The book is one of the fullest statements of the scientific basis of Philosophical Radicalism— written by the last grandchild of the *Encyclopédistes*. It expressed what may be called the central popular philosophy of republican France

251

—its materialism, its agnosticism and its meliorism. If it fell flat, the reason is not so much that it was badly written—though certainly it is neither lucid, logical nor complete—or that it is in no sense original, but that its message was no longer deeply felt by the rising generation. The dynamic force had gone out of Radicalism and had not yet attached itself to any other popular creed. The general view of Clemenceau's *magnum opus* was that of Dr. Johnson on the walking dog : " It is not done well ; but you are surprised to find it done at all." Certainly *Au Soir de la pensée* is a *tour de force*, a marvel of sustained energy and courage.

In the end those are the two words that characterize Clemenceau. No other statesman of the Third Republic survived middle age with such energy and courage ; if one had, the Third Republic itself might have survived. Clemenceau had no successor in his own country. His spiritual heir, strangely enough, is an Englishman, and a man as typically England as Clemenceau was typically France.

Between the careers of Winston Churchill and Georges Clemenceau the resemblance is extraordinary. Each began as a military correspondent, Clemenceau in the American civil war, Churchill in the Boer war. Each had a close family connection with the United States, Clemenceau through his American wife, Churchill through his American mother. Each wrote an unsuccessful novel and each made a name as a writer. The parallel can be prolonged into politics. Both had to deal with serious labour troubles early in their Cabinet careers, and both called in the troops to deal with strikers and law-breakers. Both were individualists, unable to pull in party-harness. Both had a genius for parliamentary opposition and—rare combination—for military strategy. Both seemed to have missed their marks and to be on the verge of inglorious retirement when the great opportunity came.

Clemenceau was seventy-three in 1914 ; he had broken with his party over a dozen issues and had the humiliation of seeing his old enemy Poincaré in the Presidency. Churchill was sixty-five in 1939 ; he had broken with his Party over the India Act and over European policy and had to stand impotently aside while the son of his old opponent steered the country through the rapids of appeasement. At the onset of the first World War, Clemenceau became President of the Commission of the Army ; at the onset of the second, Churchill became First Lord of the Admiralty. When defeat at the hands of the Germans seemed imminent, France in her hour of need turned to Clemenceau, Britain to Churchill. Clemenceau did for France in 1917 what Churchill was to do for Britain in 1940. Each offered blood, sweat and tears, and each galvanized his country into unity. Each dominated his Cabinet to the eclipse of his colleagues. Each paved the way to victory by means of an American alliance; each put the armies of the Western Allies under a unified command. Each concentrated on winning the war to the exclusion of considerations of reconstruction.

There is resemblance between the two characters as well as between their careers. The same impetuosity can be seen in Churchill as in Clemenceau, the same pugnacity and the same irrepressible wit—though these characteristics were more acute in the Frenchman, whom they led into a bad marriage, frequent duels and a multiplicity of personal enemies. There is the same quixotic loyalty to old friends and the same impatience with old bores. The very style of the two men is similar, each direct and personal, each conversational in debate and grandiloquent in set speeches, each with a gift of memorable—and often unrepeatable—phrase. And the parallel may perhaps be extended one stage further. Clemenceau staked his reputation on a French alliance with England ; he was greeted with derisive cries of " Aoh yes ! " Churchill made a desperate attempt at a permanent union with France ; it was rejected with an incredulous " Oh yeh ? " But the parallel must not be pushed to absurdity. The difference between the two men is greater than their resemblance—as great, in fact, as the difference between the nations they served.

254

ENVOI

Clemenceau served France prominently for fifty years and actively for nearly seventy. In his eighty-eighth year, feeling that the end could not be far away, he wrote as follows with a steady hand on a single sheet of paper :

This is my Will. I wish to be buried at Colombier, beside my father. My body will be taken from the mortuary to the burial place without any procession or ceremony of any kind. . . . Neither manifestations, nor invitations, nor rites. Round the grave, nothing but an iron grill, with no name, as in the case of my father. In my coffin I wish there to be placed my stick with the lead knob, which I had as a boy, and the small box covered in goatskin which will be found in the left corner of the top shelf of my wardrobe. There should be left in it the little book which was put there by the hand of *ma chère maman*. Two little bunches of dried flowers should be put with it ; they will be found on the mantelpiece of the room which opens on the garden. The smaller bouquet will be put in the shell-case which holds the larger, and laid beside my body.

I name my very dear friend Nicolas Piétri as executor in conjunction with Maître Pournin, advocate, and my son Michel, and I thank them for the trouble that this may give them.

Done at Paris, March 28th, 1929.

GEORGES CLEMENCEAU

In the autumn his physical energy failed. His courage remained ("Are you ill ?" he was

255

asked. " No, not ill. Only dying "), and fought its last fight till he died, on November 28th. It was at the time when Frenchmen were still applauding Poincaré, the man who had saved the franc ; they had forgotten Clemenceau, the man who had saved *la France.*

FINIS

Short Bibliography

BOOKS ON THE THIRD REPUBLIC

The best and fullest work in English is D. W. Brogan's *The Development of Modern France* (Hamish Hamilton, 1940). Beginners will find in Pierre Maillaud's *France* (Oxford University Press, 1943) a useful introduction; in Paul Vaucher's *Post-War France* (Home University Library, 1934) a survey of the years between 1918 and 1933; and in Dorothy M. Pickles' *The French Political Scene* (Nelson, 1938) a valuable sketch of the political background. The making of the Constitution is described in R. L. Middleton's *The French Political System* (Benn, 1925), and the spirit behind it in David Thomson's *Democracy in France* (Oxford University Press, 1946).

In French the standard work of reference is Volume VII of the *Histoire de France*, by E. Lavisse. The best short text-book is *La Troisième République 1870–1914* (Paris, 1939), by Georges Bourgin. For a Right-wing version of the story, see Jacques Bainville, *La Troisième République* (Paris, 1935); for a Left-wing version, A. Zévaès' *Histoire de la Troisième République* (new edition: 1938).

BOOKS ON CLEMENCEAU

Of the biographies written in or translated into English, only H. M. Hyndman's *Clemenceau : the Man and his Time* (Grant Richards, 1919) and G. Bruun's *Clemenceau* (Harvard, 1943) are worth recommending. There is a short sketch by Winston Churchill in *Great Contemporaries* (Cassell, 1935). A great deal of interesting material is to be found in Jean Martet's

CLEMENCEAU

Clemenceau : the Events of his Life as told by Himself to his Former Secretary (Longmans, 1930).

In French the fullest biography is *La Vie orgueilleuse de Clemenceau* (Paris, 1930), by Georges Suarès. *Le Ministère Clemenceau : Journal d'un témoin* (Paris, 1930), by H. Mordacq, is invaluable on the years 1917–19. For a vicious denigration see *Le Véritable Clemenceau* (Berne, 1920), by Ernest Judet. The most recent biography is *Clemenceau* (Paris, 1939), by H. Mordacq, an uncritical account which might well be supplemented by the *Clemenceau* (Paris, 1931) of Georges Michon.

BOOKS BY CLEMENCEAU

(Those marked with an asterisk have been translated in America.)

De la Génération des éléments anatomiques (1865).
La Mêlée sociale (1895).
Le Grand Pan (1896).
*Les Plus Forts (1898).
*Au Pied du Sinaï (1898).
La Voile du bonheur (1901).
*Aux Embusquades de la Vie (1903).

Collections of articles on the Dreyfus Case :
    L'Iniquité (1899).
    Vers la Réparation (1899).
    Contre la Justice (1900).
    Les Juges (1901).
    Justice militaire (1901).
    Injustice militaire (1902).
    La Honte (1903).
*Notes de Voyages dans l'Amérique du Sud (1911).
Demosthène (1926).
Au Soir de la pensée (1927).
Claude Monet : Les Nymphéas (1928).
Grandeurs et misères d'une victoire (1930).

258

Index

INDEX

INDEX

INDEX

INDEX